I0008425

Table of Contents

About book

Apache® Spark is one of the fastest growing technology in BigData computing world. It supports multiple programming languages like Java, Scala, Python and R. Hence, many existing and new framework started to integrate Spark platform as well in their platform for instance Hadoop, Cassandra, EMR etc. While creating Spark certification material HadoopExam Engineering team found that there is no proper material and book is available for the Spark (version 2.x) which covers the concepts as well as use of various features and found difficulty in creating the material. Therefore, they decided to create full length book for Spark (Databricks® CRT020 Spark Scala/Python or PySpark Certification) and outcome of that is this book. In this book technical team try to cover both fundamental concepts of Spark 2.x topics which are part of the certification syllabus as well as add as many exercises as possible and in current version we have around 46 hands on exercises added which you can execute on the Databricks community edition, because each of this exercises tested on that platform as well, as this book is focused on the PySpark version of the certification, hence all the exercises and their solution provided in the Python. This book is divided in 13 chapters, as you move ahead chapter by chapter you would be comfortable with the Databricks Spark Python certification (CRT020). Same exercises you can convert into different programming language like Java, Scala & R as well. Its more about the syntax.

Feedback

This is a full-length book from http://hadoopexam.com and we love the feedback so that we can improve the quality of the book. Please send your feedback on hadoopexam@gmail.com or admin@hadoopexam.com

Even you want to share your experience and story with the preparation of the real exam certification please share the same. It would help other candidates as well.

Restrictions

Disclaimer:

Publication Information

First Version Published: Dec 2019

Edition: 1.0

Piracy

If you come across any illegal copies of this works in any form on the Internet, then please share the detail with URL, location or website name immediately on email id hadoopexam@gmail.com we really appreciate your help in protecting author's hard work and also help in reducing the cost of material.

Author/Trainer required

Corporate Trainer: We have many requirements, where our corporate partners need their team to be trained on particular skill sets. If you are already providing corporate trainings for any skills set, then please become our onsite training partner and fill in the form mentioned above and our respective team will contact you soon. You will get very good revenue for sure. However, what we want, you must be able to train our corporate partner resources. What matters to us? Your proficiency in a particular domain/skill and good oral communication skills. You must be able to accessible to learners as well.

Online Trainer: If you are a working professional and master or proficient in any particular skills and feel that, you are capable of giving online virtual trainings e.g. 2 hrs a day until course contents are completed. Please send an email at admin@hadoopexam.com . You will get a very good revenue share for sure. What matters to us? Your proficiency in a particular domain/skill and good oral communication skills. It will certainly not impact your daily work.

Self-Paced Trainings: Ok, you want to work as per your comfortable time and at the same time sharpen your skills. You can consider this option. You can create self-paced trainings on particular domain/skills. Please send an email at admin@hadoopexam.com with us as soon as possible. Before somebody else connect with us for the same skill set. Your commitment is very important for us. We respect your work and we will not sell your work in just $10 or less to acquire more resources. As we know, it takes a good amount of time and you will provide quality material, so we charge reasonable on that so, you will feel motivated with your work and effort. We respect you and your skill.

Certification Material: You may be already certified professional or preparing for particular certification in a specific domain/skill. So why not use this to make money as well as sharing your effort with other learners globally. Please connect with us by filling form or send email at admin@hadoopexam.com and our respective team will contact you soon.

Author: Yes, we are also looking for authors. Who can write books on a particular technology and what you can get certainly a very good revenue sharing and you can bring the same on your resume or linked in profile to show your excellence? Yes, we are not in need of very good oral communication skills, but good writing skill. However, team will also help you to get work done. Author can be more than one for a particular book. However, we wanted you to be in long relationship. So that you don't just write a single e book, but can create an entire series for a particular domain or skill. Good royalty for sure...

Trending Skills (Not limited these):

Hadoop	EMC	Adobe	Data	Infrastructre
Spark	NetApp	Alfresco	Analysis	Automation
AWS	VMWare	Apple	DJango	Internet of
Cloud	CISCO	AppSense	Docker	Things (IOT)
Azure	HP	AutoDesk	Drupal	ISO
Cloud			Graphics	Development
Google				Java
Cloud				Java Script
JQuery	Mobile	IBM Watson	Scala	SAP
Kali Linux	Application	IBM BPM	Python	SAS
Laravel	Development	WebMethod	Java	Salesforce
Linux	NodeJS	Gemfire	SQL/PLSQL	Oracle Cloud
Machine	Android	Liferay	Ruby	Redhat
Learning	Angular JS			
	Arduino			

Chapter-1: CRT020 Databricks® certified Associate Developer using Python or PySpark

Access Source code: As this book has around 46 hands on exercises and you wanted to download the same. Link for downloading the source code is provided before the start of each chapter, wherever it is required. From chapter-6 onwards we would be doing hands-on exercises.

Access to Certification Preparation Material
I have already purchased this book printed version from open market, I still wanted to get access for the certification preparation material offered by HadoopExam.com, do you provide any discount for the same.

First of all, thanks for considering the learning material from HadoopExam.com. Yes, we certainly consider your subscription request and you are eligible for discount as well. What you have to do is that, you can send receipt this book purchase and our sales team can offer you 10% discount on the preparation material. Please send an email to hadoopexam@gmail.com or admin@hadoopexam.com with the purchase detail and your requirement

---

Why Spark framework is so popular

Apache Spark is one of the fastest growing technology for the Data processing, Data Analytics, Machine Learning, Graph Processing and Data Science. Reason for its adoption in the industry are various for example on the macro levels we can say, it has:

- There are many organizations which supports the Spark in production like Cloudera, Databricks, MapR, Microsoft, IBM, Datastax etc.
- Newly Dataframe based API is very developer friendly, mainly after the release of Spark 2.x
- Spark supports already popular programming languages like Scala (Spark framework, itself written using Scala), Java, Python and R. Hence, companies do not have to train developer for specific programming language if they are already having resources with any of these programming skills and

they have to learn various other aspects of
the Spark framework.
- Support of Structured Query Language, most
of the Data Analytics/engineer already well
versed with the SQL. And Spark also supports
very well the same SQL syntax.
- Frequent releases with the new features and
enhancements.
- Much faster processing engine compare to
any other available Data processing engine.

There are many other things which make the Spark
very popular technology. These are few of the
reason, for which you have selected this book and
CRT020 certification exam.

Introduction to CRT020 Certification

As demand is growing day by day for the Spark
Developer and industry wants easy access to Spark
professional and for searching right candidates,
they don't have to spend so much time. To find the
resources which are good or have some knowledge
of the Spark framework and from the candidate
side, it should also be easy to prove by showing that
he is already a certified professional in Spark
technology. There are various Spark certifications
but CRT020 became very popular recently because

this is conducted by the company called Databricks, who heavily spend their time on the Spark framework development as well as they have their own enterprise version of the Spark framework with the additional enterprise feature. Databricks is conducting Spark certification since many years and they have different certifications for Python and Scala programming language, and to pass this certification you have to have fundamental knowledge about how Spark works and similarly have good experience for doing hands on with the Spark. Therefore, it is recommended you complete all the exercises given in this book as well as in the certification preparation material provided by HadoopExam.com . In next few sections we would be discussing about the frequently asked questions for Spark2.x CRT020 certification.

Where and How to get Databricks Spark CRT020 Certification Sample Questions

There are various Spark certification exams available and this particularly this one "CRT020 : Databricks Certified Associate Developer for Apache Spark 2.4 and Scala 2.11 - Assessment Certification Exam " is the latest available Spark exam from the Databricks and similarly Python version. This certification became popular in very short span of time and within the launch on HadoopExam.com , more than 100 learners have subscribed in a week. This proves that, how popular is this certification exam. And also this is based and tested on the Databricks community edition of the platform.

Even it uses the Databricks community edition but its underline engine is same as Apache Spark, hence, the same code you can run on the Apache Spark as well as on Databricks Spark platform.

However, it is recommended that you practice very well before you appear in the real exam. Because without practice, you would not be able to complete the exam on time. CRT020 exam is divided in two major section as below.

- Multiple Choice Questions (Get access to all 200+ Multiple Choice Questions for Scala & PySpark)
- Assessment (Hands On Section) : Get access to all 40+ assessment Questions and Answer (Including Videos) Scala or PySpark We are continuously updating the material which are available online.

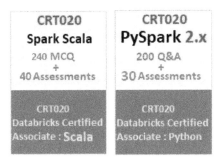

CRT020	CRT020
Spark Scala	**PySpark 2.x**
240 MCQ	200 Q&A
+	+
40 Assessments	30 Assessments
CRT020 Databricks Certified Associate : Scala	CRT020 Databricks Certified Associate : Python

If you want to check the Sample Questions and Answer then use the below link or watch the below video to understand more.

- Scala : http:#hadoopexam.com/spark/databricks/SparkScalaCRT020DatabricksAssessment.html
- PySpark : http:#hadoopexam.com/spark/databricks/PySparkCRT020DatabricksAssessment.html
- Sample Assessment PySpark: http:#learn.hadoopexam.com/PySparkCRT020/SampleAssessment/index.html
- Sample Assessment Scala : http:#learn.hadoopexam.com/SparkScalaCRT020/SampleAssessment/index.html
- Multiple Choice:

http:#learn.hadoopexam.com/SparkScalaCRT020/Sample/index.html

How you should prepare for CRT020 Spark Scala/Python (Databricks) Certification Exam?

Databricks is the leader for Apache Spark technology, they support the open source version of Apache Spark framework.

Based on the open source Apache Spark, Databricks created enterprise version of Spark Framework. And this newly created framework also works on the Cloud platform like AWS, Azure, Google cloud etc.

Since last few years Databricks platform became very popular because they are capable of deploying Spark in the production env. Companies which are using Databricks platform in production or planning to have in production in need of Databricks certified professionals. Databricks has following two popular certifications as of today. They might come up with more in future for different solutions like Machine Learning, Graph and Structure Streaming etc. Let's go through below two links for the currently available certifications.

- CRT020 : Databricks Certified Associate Developer Apache Spark 2.4 with Scala 2.11 : Assessment Certification
- CRT020 : Databricks Certified Associate Developer for Apache Spark 2.4 with Python 3.0 - Assessment Certification

Both the above certification exam has the same pattern and syllabus. Only difference is, which programming language you prefer.

Exam format: In each certification exam there are two sections as below

- **Multiple choice** questions and answers (which include single and multiple correct answers, fill in the blanks questions and short answers etc.)
- **Assessment Exam:** You need to write complete solution for given problem statements or some initial code would be provided. If there is any data required, they would already providing you the path of the stored data.

However, it is not mentioned on the certification detail page that how many questions they would be asking in each section. HadoopExam.com experience and feedback received from learner shows that there would be around 20 multiple choice questions and 20+ assessment exercises would be given and difficulty level would increases Question by Question, Same is provided on HadoopExam online Spark Certification Simulator. It is clearly mentioned that the exam would be 3 hrs long and include both the above section. Hence, please note that

- In multiple choice 20 questions would be covered. In that they would be asking various concepts, internal Architecture, API and SQL functions-based questions.
- Around 20 assessment questions would be asked, in this you would be given problem statement for each question and you need to write or implement the solutions either using PySpark or Spark Scala.
- You need to write problem solution in online version of Databricks Enterprise platform.
- **How the Scoring would be done?** Databricks have not mentioned, whether you need to pass separately each exam section or aggregate score from both the section would be considered. What HadoopExam.com experience again says that you need to score

75% marks in each section at least so that your overall aggregated score remains 75% as well and you can clear the exam. Whether Databricks consider individual section or aggregated marks.

Timeline for CRT020 Spark Certification preparation

Preparations and timeline depend on the how good you are in Spark technology as well as what is your strength in Scala and Python programming language. As per HadoopExam.com experience following timeline you can consider for preparing this certification, if you spend 2-3 hrs. 5 days a week.

- **6 months:** If you are completely new to Spark.
- **3-4 month** : If you know one of the programming language like Java, Scala, or Python etc.
- **1-2 month**: If you already know Spark technology.
- Above timeline is not perfect these are derived based on HadoopExam.com previous experience with other certifications or based on the feedback received from the learners.

How to prepare for CRT020 Spark Certification

To prepare for the Spark certification you need to have right material, and also you need to properly planned and have properly drafted material, which can save your lot of time. Otherwise, you would be going for material here and there and lose lot of time and which may take much longer to complete the exam even without having full confidence in the real exam. Also, remember if things are not properly planned and drafted or organized, it does not matter how good you are in Spark.

To make your life simple and easy for the Spark CRT020 certification preparation HadoopExam.com have created cool material. You should consider the following material for preparing Spark Certification

1. CRT020 : Databricks Certified Associate Developer Apache Spark 2.4 with Scala 2.11 : Assessment Certification : Include 200+ multiple choice questions and more than 40 assessments.
2. CRT020 : Databricks Certified Associate Developer for Apache Spark 2.4 with Python 3.0 - Assessment Certification : Include 200+

multiple choice questions and more than 30 assessments. More would be added soon.

3. Apache Spark Professional Training with Hands On Lab Sessions
4. Spark 2.X SQL (Using Scala) Professional Training with Hands On Sessions
5. PySpark 2.X (Using Python) Professional Training with Hands On Sessions
6. Scala Professional Training with HandsOn Session
7. Python Professional Training with HandsOn Session

All the required questions come with the full explanation and answer, to justify the correctness of the answer.

- It covers the entire syllabus for both Python and Scala version of certification exam. You can attempt questions and answers as many times as you want.
- All multiple-choice question and answer, you can access from any device where browsers are supported like Desktop, Macbook/IOS, iPhone, mobile, tablet etc.
- There are no separate installations are required.

- Most of our learners are happy that because while travelling or during free time they can access the certification preparation material as well as interview questions audio cum video book.
- You can check some sample questions and answers using below link.

  - Check Sample Assessment Paper **(Scala)**
  - Check Multiple Choice Sample Paper(Scala)
  - Check Sample Assessment Paper **(Python)**
  - Check Multiple Choice Sample Paper (Python)
  - Spark 2.x Interview Preparations (Total 185+ Interview Questions): Video + Audio + PDF

More detail on assessment exam

HadoopExam.com give capability to you for accessing problem statement and assessment solutions which can be accessed from mobile and tablet and that you can understand the same in detail. Once you understand the problem statement, then in the next tab, you would be given instructions to access or download the data which you need to use for solving the problem statement.

Videos: Possibly for selected assessment would have videos as well as, author would explain the entire problem statements and its solution. However, it is not guaranteed that each assessment would be having the videos.

Assessment Solution: We are providing step by step solution for the given problem in multiple steps. Each step would be written with the detailed comments as well. So that you can easily understand what is being done in the solution.

Training: HadoopExam.com has very popular training for Apache Spark, Spark SQL, Structured Streaming in Python and Scala. As well as interview Questions Audio cum video books. These all are On-Demand training access which you can access anytime anywhere using mobile, desktop, MacBook, iPhone etc. Check all below and more material would be added soon.

Spark Interview Preparation

By going through certification exam and training, your ultimate target is to join the companies which are using these new platforms or if you are already working in the organization then you are looking for vertical growth or increase on pay package and salary. Hence, HadoopExam.com prepared almost 185+ Interview Questions and answers which you can access in these two formats eBook and Video cum Audio Book format. This material if you want to read you can read, you want to watch you can watch and if you want to listen then you can listen as well anytime-anywhere. Check more detail as below

Chapter-2: FAQ for Spark CRT020 Certification

Spark CRT020 Certifications FAQ (43 FAQs)

Question-1: I am a Java programmer, which language I have to choose for this CRT020 Spark certification?

Answer: As you know currently there is no specific certification in Java programming language for Spark. But Spark fully support Java programming language. Spark framework is written using the Scala framework and the Scala itself uses Java Run time environment. Hence, you should be quite comfortable with the Spark CRT020 certification using Scala framework.

Question-2: I already know the Python programming then which version should I choose for CRT020?

Answer: In this case your obvious choice would be PySpark CRT020 certification.

Question-3: I don't know Python programming language, is it required to be an expert in Python to work on the Spark Framework using Python?

Answer: No, we don't think so. If you know the basics of Python and you are fluent in one of the programming languages then it is good enough. You can attend crash courses for Scala and Python on HadoopExam to learn the same.

Question-4: I prefer Python, do you have material specific the Python or PySpark?

Answer: Yes, this book you are reading has both the version Spark Certification using Scala and Using PySpark. So, you can choose as per your requirement. Similarly, all the practice material created on the HadoopExam are also segregated based on the programming language.

Question-5: How many questions are expected in the real exam, as I see HadoopExam has around 200+ practice questions and around 40 assessments?

Answer: We are providing practice questions which are based on the feedback provided by the learners and expertise of our engineering team. And we want you to practice as much as possible before your real exam. In real exam, based on our learners feedback you will get

- Around 20 multiple choice questions (included fundamentals concepts as well as some programming questions)
- Around 20 assessments, which you need to complete on the Databricks community edition provided in the Cloud env.

Question-6: What is your recommendation regarding spending time on multiple choice questions and assessment questions?

Answer: HadoopExam recommend that you should be able to complete all multiple-choice questions and answer in less than 25 mins.

As assessment questions can take more time, so spend around 2 hr 30 mins on assessment. You can see there are around 20 assessment questions.

Question-7: Do you know how is marking done between multiple choice and assessment questions?

Answer: No, as of now we don't know. But it seems assessment questions would have more weightage. However, we still don't recommend skipping multiple choice questions at all.

Question-8: What is your recommendation during the real exam for attempting the questions?

Answer: It is similar to any other exam which you have appeared till now. Always attempt easier questions first and then do all the tough questions once you are done with easy questions. If you got stuck on a particular question then don't spend too much time on it and try to attempt another easy question. This is universally known strategy. But yes, for this CRT020 certification exam complete all multiple-choice questions first in less than 25 mins.

Question-9: Is multiple choice questions had more than one answer correct?

Answer: Till now, whatever feedback we have received. All multiple-choice questions are having only single correct answer, but it is not guaranteed for future exam. Because Databricks has not explicitly mentioned it.

Question-10: Is it mandatory to attempt multiple choice question first and then coding question?

Answer: No, it is not mandatory in CRT020 certification exam. But we recommend you spend your initial time on multiple choice. Because once you start assessment question and then coming back to multiple choice question is little hard. However, it is allowed to switch between these two sections.

Question-11: Is there any specific section from which multiple-choice questions are being asked?

Answer: Again, this is not mentioned specifically on the exam guide. But we have seen more questions are being asked to check your understanding of the Spark fundamentals and the topic mentioned on the first 4 section are frequently being asked in the multiple-choice questions.

Question-12: Still can you specify which section; we need to prepare specifically for multiple choice questions?

Answer: Ok, for that you should consider the following sections

- What is the use of Spark Driver component?
- What is the relation between core and executor?
- How executor and tasks are related
- What do you mean by partitioning and how Spark parallel processing affected by partitioning?

- Understand these three components working in detail
    1. Jobs
    2. Stages
    3. Tasks
- And how all these are related to each other.
- What is the caching, and how it can be implemented?
- You would certainly get multiple choice question based on caching and memory management.
- Understand the Spark architecture
- Make yourself well aware about wide and narrow transformation.

Question-13: How complex or tough to resolve assessment question and answer?

Answer: We have seen that out of 20, around 6-7 questions are quite easy. And 3-4 questions are time consuming and little hard as well. And rest are medium level. If you have completed all the exercises from this book and Spark practice material then you will feel this exam is quite easy to crack. Even after completing all the assessment, we are sure that you are quite comfortable working using the Spark framework.

Question-14: Do you think we should cover each individual topic mentioned in the syllabus for the CRT020 certification?

Answer: As you can see syllabus is quite wide compare to any other certification. And you should not skip any section from the syllabus before the real exam. In some situation, if you have not done 1 or 2 section from the entire syllabus that is ok. But don't skip more than 1 or 2 topics mentioned in the syllabus. We are also doing hard work for your success then why do you want to skip any section, lets complete all before your real exam.

Question-15: Can you please provide the detail, what kind of questions are being asked for the assessments?

Answer: Regarding the kind of assessment questions, you would be asked questions like below but not limited, again complete all the questions and answer from this book as well as practice material provide by HadoopExam.com

- Load the data from file (most frequently asked parquet, JSON) and possibly other format as well like text, csv. Each exam attempt has different questions and answer.
- Create DataFrame and extract the data from it by applying projection or filter

- De-duplicate the data
- Find the distinct records from the DataFrame
- Transform the DataFrame by applying Lambda functions.
- Finally write the data to the file store like in Parquet, JSON or text format.
- Make yourself comfortable with the following file formats in order of priority
    1. Parquet
    2. JSON
    3. CSV
    4. Text

Question-16: I am already certified with Spark 1.6, what is your recommendation for this certification preparation?

Answer: Its good, then for preparing for this certification is even easier for you. Because the API in Spark 2.x is much easier to use compare to RDD API.

Question-17: I am already certified in Spark 1.6, why should I go for Spark CRT020 certification?

Answer: Spark had done a major change in Spark 2.x and most of the API is re-written to support for

- Project Tungsten
- Catalyst optimizer

And you should know all this, if you are building your career with the Spark technology. And there are many more new things, we highly recommend that you always update your certification credentials. As in Spark 1.6 major focus was on RDD, DStream and this is not at all recommended in Spark 2.x for programming but rather you should use Spark SQL framework heavily for ETL, Data analytics workload.

Question-18: Is Structured Streaming and Machine learning being asked in the real exam?

Answer: No, only the things which are explicitly mentioned for the syllabus, is being asked in the exam.

Question-19: is CRT020 asks questions based on RDD API?

Answer: No, in the real exam, you don't have questions based on RDD API. However, you should know how an RDD can be converted into DataFrame.

Question-20: Should we memorize the Spark API for CRT020 exam?

Answer: As on the exam instructions it is mentioned that you would be provided with the API doc and you can search the same during you real exam. But HadoopExam highly recommend that all frequently used API and packages you remember & memorize, so that you don't have to waste your time on finding the required methods from the docs. However, make yourself comfortable with the API doc as well, before the exam.

Question-21: Is HadoopExam providing any specific notes for memorizing the API for this certification exam?

Answer: As of now we don't have, but in some time we would have. That would be exclusively available for the learners who have subscription on our online material on HadoopExam.com . You can keep visiting release and update tab on the website.

Question-22: Do you recommend which pages we should have try and make myself comfortable.

Answer: for **Python** use below

1. https://spark.apache.org/docs/latest/api/python/pyspark.sql.html
2. https://docs.databricks.com/

For **Scala** use below

1. https://spark.apache.org/docs/latest/api/scala/org.apache.spark.sql.package

In this check API related to below components

- DataFrame

- Row
- DataFrameReader
- DataFrameWriter
- Column

Question-23: I am good at Spark SQL; can I avoid using DataFrame at all in the exam?

Answer: In the exam you would see most of the questions are based on the DataFrame and initial code snippet also they are giving using DataFrame. So, try to solve using DataFrame first, if not comfortable then switch the Spark SQL API. It may eat some of your time.

Question-24: Where should I practice this exam. HadoopExam provide any environment for practicing the questions?

Answer: No, HadoopExam does not provide any environment for practicing coding question. You can use the Databricks community edition for the same. (We would be providing the videos, how you can use the same). If it is currently not available then soon it would be released.

Question-25: How long does Databricks take to announce the result?

Answer: Initially, user was complaining that they are not getting the result until one week. But we have seen recently learners are getting their result on the same day. If not same day, then within 2-3 days they are announcing the result.

Question-26: Are you sure 20-25 mins are good enough for multiple choice questions?

Answer: Most of our learners who had practiced well, completing multiple choice section in less than 20 mins. So please read contents from the book carefully before your real exam.

Question-27: My friend was saying that coding questions in the CRT020 exam are tough?

Answer: These questions are not very tough, few questions you may feel tough. If you have not practiced well, if you know the stuff then questions are not that tough. Yes, that is possible that data processing or understanding the data may take more time for you.

Question-28: Why people say, keep Spark API by heart for this CRT020 exam?

Answer: As we suggested before, because we have seen learners are not able to complete the assessment exam on time. Because they spend more time on the documentation. We are again suggesting please memorize the API as much as possible, specially the things which are frequently used. Like Row, DataFrame, Select, filter, distinct, foreach, take, persist, format, load, StructType, StructField etc.

Memorize how to set the properties like "spark.sql.shuffle.partions" how it is set on SparkSession or SparkContext. Soon HadoopExam would be creating quick reference or revision notes the same and would be available through online subscription only.

Question-29: Is there really time-pressure in the exam?

Answer: Simple rule, if you take pressure then certainly it is. If you don't take pressure and calmly go through each question it is fine. Even you don't know the API search in the doc (use CTRL+F for browser search and find specific keyword etc.)., always keep document opened in another tab of the browser, so you can immediately check the doc as well, if required. Have patience during the exam and calmly appear in it.

Question-30: Can I do copy paste from the API documentation?

Answer: No, you cannot do any copy paste. Because this feature is disabled in the real exam.

Question-31: Is question in exam are independent or dependent?

Answer: All questions are independent.

Question-32: I have some feedback and information about the Spark certification which needs to be updated here, for the benefits of the other learners?

Answer: Feedback is always welcome, this book and most of our material is being updated based on the feedback we receive from our learners. You can provide your feedback by sending an email on the hadoopexam@gmail.com or admin@hadoopexam.com

Question-33: Do we expect any question related to GraphFrame in the certification exam?

Answer: No, although GraphFrame is depend on the DataFrame and uses the same execution engine as used by the SparkSQL. But as of now in this certification we don't see any question is being asked on the GraphFrame or data processing using Graphs.

Question-34: Why Spark technology in so much news?

Answer: From the Apache it is one of the most actively worked framework. In recent years BigData, Real time Data processing, Artificial

Intelligence and many other things pushed high. And all this need a processing engine which can process such things efficiently. Even Hadoop MapReduce which become suddenly popular, is being replaced by Spark computation engine. There are almost more than 1000 contributors on the open source platform.

After Spark 2.0, it is very easy to learn. Its API is very intuitive as well if you are good at SQL queries then API/SQL makes it much easier for you to learn. If you are a programmer than DataFrame API would help you a lot for working with the Spark.

There are many organizations who had pushed Spark applications in the production. Which proves the quality and reliability of the Spark framework.

Companies already having Hadoop cluster do not have to create separate Spark cluster. They can use their existing framework for the running Spark applications on the same cluster. Whether it is written using Java/Scala/Python or R language.

Always having new technologies knowledge will give you the opportunity to draw more salary. And less chance of job loss. You can switch your career and Spark is one of them for sure.

Question-35: I have good knowledge of Spark, and almost 3+ years' experience working with Spark, why should I go for certification?

Answer: There is a myth in IT industry that certification does not help in career. This is not at all true. Having certification certainly helps in following ways

- You will know all the hidden features of a technology. If you go for certification
- It shows your career focus
- While resume shortlisting, it is given priority (Because first shortlisting is done by recruitment team, they don't have enough knowledge about technology. Hence, they look for your credentials in the resume).
- First impression on the interviewer.
- Interviewer will focus on things which you have written in resume.
- You will be classified in a separate category.
- It will give you confidence during the interview and while working in the organization.
- So, avoid all the people who have -ve thinking about learning. Learning can never be costly and time wasting (universal truth).
- Certainly, it's an additional feather in your hat.
- There are many other latent benefits for doing certification.

Question-36: Do you give priority to specific vendor for Spark?

Answer: No, we don't give priority to any vendor. It varies based on many factors.

- Like if you wanted to get certified in both Hadoop and Spark then go for Cloudera Hadoop and Spark certification. And you have to have knowledge how to use Cloudera platform.
- If you are working on MapR platform then you can go for MapR Spark certification. Even other advantage is that MapR Spark certification is not as lengthy as Databricks Spark certification. You can prepare for MapR Spark certification in quite less time. You can see pros and cons that Databricks is more involved with the Spark and really tough one among the all Spark certification.
- Hortonworks Spark certification: This is again Hands on certification for the Spark. And have limited syllabus and specific objectives are given. Recently updated to include and support Spark 2.x version on the Hortonworks HDP platform.

However, while writing this book, we have seen most of the vendors are upgrading their certifications to accommodate Spark 2.x

Question-37: I don't know both Scala and Python then which programming language you would recommend?

Answer: It is very tricky question to answer. We recommend learn both the programming language. These are beautiful language to work upon. But based on the following career path you can choose respective programming language.

Scala:

- Java programmer should go for this
- If you want to become Data Engineer than go for this
- If you want to work on Data Cleaning and collecting Data than go for this.
- If you already know Java/Scala than go for this

Python:

- If you know Python than go for PySpark.
- If you are on Business Analytics profile go for PySpark

- I want to become Data Scientist, you can use either PySpark or Scala Spark

It should not be considered based on the fact that Spark is written in Scala, so I should give preference to Spark Scala. Not at all true after Spark 2.x version.

Question-38: During the certification preparation, I am also preparing for the interview, can you please let me know, is there any material for the same?

Answer: yes, we do have interview preparation material for the Spark. Which you can get it from here. This is part of our premium and pro subscription.

Question-39: What is the proctor during real exam?

Answer: During your real exam there is one person who take care your real exam environment preparation as well as keep an eye on you. However, keep in mind that proctor is not only for keeping an eye on you but he or she is there to help you. If you find any issue with the connectivity, accessing material, checking time and any other status about the exam environment. They all are well trained for all these stuffs and very helpful.

You can start the exam 15 mins earlier than scheduled start time and proctor would ask you to show the desk and your place with the 360-degree using the webcam installed on either laptop or desktop. During the exam hours your desktop remain in sharing mode. It is always recommended you start 15 mins earlier than your scheduled time. You should always have a bigger monitor for your exam and avoid very small laptop screen and recommended size is 1600X900.

Question-40: Can I prepare CRT020 Spark Certification in two weeks?

Answer: Yes, it is possible. You need to spend around 4-6 hrs. daily on the training and you should solve and understand all questions provided by HadoopExam.com then you are ready to take this exam. However, it all depend on you. How much you have grasped and understood the stuff from the preparation material. Many of our learners completed this exam in less than 30 days. So, you can also do the same.

Question-41: Performance of the environment

Answer: Cluster provided in the cloud may not be performant but good enough for solving the given tasks. Hence, you have to be very careful when you submit any tasks and your solution must not involve the shuffle phase with huge volume of data.

Because most of our learners have given the feedback that the cluster provided during the exam is very slow. However, since then it is improved and recently candidates are not facing this issue. There are occurrences where learners face the session disconnected issues during the exam, you may also be ready for such issues and it can be because of

- Your internet connection is not good
- Proctor internet connection is not good
- Cloud environment may not be reachable

Once your session got disconnected and connected back then you need to inform the proctor and he/she may deduct this time from your overall time. It all depend on the proctor discretion. If you belong to a country where internet connection reliability is challenging then make sure during your exam it does not happen.

Question-42: Do you see any issue related to the size of the data, given in exam?

Answer: Not all tasks you would be given with the huge data. But rather smaller DataFrame would be given. However, out of all the tasks couple of tasks would involve huge data. And that may become challenging and time consuming as well. Data may contain 100's of parameters or columns in a csv file. You need to remove all the unwanted columns and apply join, filter and saving your final result. It is always recommended that all the easy questions should be attempted first and then go for high volume data. Because the cluster given to you most likely single node and not good enough for huge volume of the data.

Question-43: Is it require to write complete application during real exam?

Answer: Many of you know that if you are writing Spark application using Scala, then you should have bundled that application using Scala Build Tool (SBT) or using Apache Maven. But this is not expected from you during the exam. Because this certification exam is not for build tool but rather testing your programming knowledge on the Spark framework.

Question-44: What is Difficulty level of the real exam?

Answer: From the learners feedback we come to know that this exam is not very difficult. Also, the task you would be performing are not administratively complex. If you have been working for 3-4 months on Spark and well-practiced all the assessment or questions then this exam you would feel very simple. Because HadoopExam added few of the hard/complex exercises as well in all these practice questions.

If you have not practiced well then, this certification exam seems very difficult and you would not be able to complete the exercise in 3 hrs. If you have practice well then, most likely you would be able to complete real exam within 3 hrs.

Many of the learners are coming to HadoopExam and told us they have good knowledge of the Spark and few tasks they completed before appearing in the real exam, but they are not able to complete the exam on time. Which proves that practice before the real exam is necessary and this is again universal truth for all the exams.

Question-45: I am working in Spark from many years and I know RDD API well, what should I use in exam?

Answer: Many of our learners are getting confused with the RDD API is being part of the syllabus. And as a programmer it is always recommended to you by the Spark community that you should avoid using the RDD in your program if you are already on the Spark 2.x or later version and should use the SparkSQL API or DataFrame API.

Yes, that is true as much as possible you should avoid using RDD in your program, if you are already using Spark 2.x version.

You should try to avoid using RDD API if possible, in your program until and unless it is absolutely necessary, for example with the broadcast variable and accumulator you have to use this.

Cloudera Hadoop and Spark Developer Certifications:

Cloudera is a pioneer for Hadoop framework and they have lot of frameworks for BigData paradigm. Cloudera provide one of the mostly used Hadoop Framework and known as CDH (Cloudera Hadoop Distribution). CDH is bundle of various big data software and one of them is Spark. Cloudera also focuses on Spark for data processing rather than traditional MapReduce frameworks. Hence, they are also delivering Spark software as part of their CDH distribution. Cloudera has various certifications for Hadoop and BigData professionals. For the Spark developer one of the most popular certifications since last 2 yrs. is been this CCA175 (Cloudera Hadoop and Spark Developer certification)

In this certification 30%-40% focus on Spark and remaining part is Hadoop Data Processing.

How to prepare for CCA175?
On http://www.HadoopExam.com this is the certification preparation material which is most subscribed among many top 10 certifications. HadoopExam provide a combined package for preparing CCA175 which include below three products.

- Spark Professional Training. with Hanson Session
- Hadoop Professional Training with Hands-on Session
- CCA175 Spark and Hadoop Developer Certifications (Includes 111 Solved Scenarios and Complimentary videos for selected solutions)

MapR Spark Certifications
The *MapR Certified Spark Developer* credential proves that you have ability to use Spark to work

with large DataFrames to perform analytics on streaming data. This credential measures your understanding of the Spark API to perform basic machine learning or SQL tasks on a given DataFrames.

This material is available on http://www.HadoopExam.com

- **Trainings**: If you are not familiar and having average experience of the Spark frameworks than we recommend below trainings which will help you prepare for these certifications
  - Apache Spark Professional (Include 2.x latest Version setup) Training with Hands on Lab
  - Spark 2.X SQL (Using Scala) Professional Training with Hands on Sessions
  - Scala Professional Training with Hands-on Session
  - Scala Professional Training with Hands-on Session

Practice Questions and Answers: To save time and focused approach for Spark certifications you should go through the below certification material

- About MapR MCSD: MapR® Certified Spark Developer: Total 220+ Solved Questions: Recently updated based on learners feedback.

Why Cloudera CCA175 Hadoop and Spark developer certification is more popular?

No doubt that Cloudera is one of the Pioneer and leader for the big data technology. And Cloudera really created the market for big data and also did very good job for Hadoop framework.

Similarly in case of Hadoop and Spark certification CCA175 Cloudera not only evaluate the Spark technology but also evaluate the Hadoop skill. And you have to solve all the given problem on Cloudera cloud-based platform.

The reason why most of the companies are looking for professional with Cloudera CCA175 Hadoop and Spark developer certification, because they have already deployed Cloudera enterprise platform in the production environment, companies in the domain like investment banks healthcare IT companies, retail E-Commerce companies, airline and travel platform, start-up which are working on data science research projects as well as machine learning solutions.

There's another reason, like Hadoop can be easily deployed on cloud platform for example AWS, Azure etc.

There is another feather recently added by merging Cloudera and Hortonworks together to lead the big data technology world.

The reason why Cloudera always remain leader because we have seen it continuously accepts new technology and update their platform very frequently compared to any other provider. For example Cloudera have adopted recent version of spark as well. They have very good support for hive, pig, OoZie, and their own develop solution Impala which can run much faster than hive.

These are the only few reason and there are much more which made Cloudera platform very popular in the big data world.

So in CCA175 exam Cloudera evaluate your skills based on 8 to 10 problems solutions which you need to solve using Hadoop Hive Pig and Spark (you can use either 1.x or 2.x version of Spark, its up to you). Cloudera is really not worried what technology you use to solve a problem but rather they want problem should be solved efficiently. Whether you use map-reduce, Hive, Impala or shell script for cleaning up the data. There would be at least three to four exercises on Apache Spark, in that they would give you already implemented some solution in the form of template and you need to fill in the remaining part using the functional programming either in Python or Scala. It is clearly said by the Cloudera that questions template would not be given in both python and Scala language for the assessment. It is up to you whether you want to write entire program your own or you want to use existing skeleton (template) provided by the Cloudera during the exam. Hence it is expected you are very good on the Apache Spark Core as well as Spark SQL at least.

This exam has higher value because it evaluates both the Hadoop and Spark in single certification exam. Complete name of the exam is CCA175 Spark and Hadoop developer. Where CCA means Cloudera Certified Associate. You can check the entire syllabus here on this page where we have provided the detailed description as well. If you have been given 10 problem statement in the real exam then at least seven problem statement you have to solve completely to clear the exam. We have seen most of our learners have scored around 9 to 10 problem solutions comfortably in the given time slot. We got the feedback that without practicing all the material provided by the HadoopExam.com you would not be able to complete the exam on time. As well as learners are able to complete the exam with the correct solutions and we are happy to share with you the same things. HadoopExam.com is providing Cloudera certification preparation material since last 6 years and our technical team had good expertise on that.

Currently the cost for this certification exam is 295 dollar, but we have seen sometime Cloudera give good discount on the fee as well or some companies have purchased coupon in bulk.

Other than this, what we have seen Impala and Hive mostly used to solve problem. For Spark they provide the skeleton for the problem scenario and you can use either Scala or python to solve the given problem. Skeleton would be provided only in one of the languages like Python or Scala. If you know Scala and Cloudera provided skeleton in

Scala, you may use this skeleton to complete the program, it may help you save the time during the exam. However, it is not mandatory that you use the skeleton provided rather you can completely write entire program from scratch.

As most of learners use the HadoopExam.com preparation material and with this practice material they are comfortably completing the exam on time or before and scoring around 9 to 10 questions perfectly.

Now how do you get this preparation material for CCA175 certification? Use the below link to get respective material
Use this 90+ solved scenario for Cloudera CCA 175 Spark and Hadoop developer certification.

1. In this material you would be provided instruction to setup the environment for practicing all scenarios.
2. Instruction would be provided to get the data for practicing the questions.
3. Step by step solution is provided for each problem statement.
4. for selected and complicated problem scenarios, videos are also provided and trainer would explain problem and solution in detail.

5. If you want to understand more on that then watch the below video.

Cloudera CCA175, Hortonworks HDPCD & Databricks CRT020 Certification Exam
There are various Spark Certification available as below and these very popular IT certification

1. Databricks Spark Certification for Developer CRT020 in Scala or Python.
2. Cloudera CCA175 Hadoop & Spark Developer in either Scala or Python.
3. Hortonworks Spark (HDPCD) certification in Scala & Python
4. MapR Spark Developer certification in Scala only.

All above certification has equal value, respective certification importance increases when based on the company in which you are working or giving interview and which platform this company is using.

For example, if company has the Cloudera platform already deployed in production then CCA175 certification exam would be more useful and certainly have more value addition then other company certifications. Similarly, if company had deployed Databricks platform in production then your Databricks Spark CRT020 certification would have more values.

Training institutes certification does not have that high importance because these institutes does not take any protected exam like above company and as soon as you pay the high amount of fee, you are entitled to get the certificate of training attended. It does not matter whether student learned in the training or attended training or not. Institute really does not evaluate the candidate's expertise. Hence, company does not consider them until and unless you have valid certification from global companies like Cloudera, Databricks, Hortonworks, MapR etc. Even experience says, students are more grilled during the interview if they write local training institutes training in their resume.

About Global certification from above companies

- Cloudera CCA175 => Spark (Either Scala or Python) + Hadoop
- Databricks Spark CRT020 => Spark Core + Spark SQL in Scala or Python
- HDPCD Spark => Spark Core + Spark SQL + Spark Structured Streaming (Either Python or Scala)

As you can see in above Cloudera CCA175 certification both Hadoop and Spark would be accessed. Hence, their syllabus would be covering two wider domains. However, the level of exam difficulty is moderate and not very tough. Most of our students have score either 9 or 10 questions correctly in the real exam. They have prepared using HadoopExam CCA175 certification simulator.

Get all the Questions for CCA175 Hadoop & Spark Certification from here

Chapter-3: Introduction to Spark 2.x

Major Changes in Spark 2.0

Databricks certified associate developer for Apache Spark currently being tested using Spark 2.4 release, which contains major changes adopted after Spark 2 release. Following things changed in Summary. Spark SQL in detail explained in Spark SQL Cookbook created by HadoopExam.com

Catalysts Optimizer: SparkSQL was developed since Spark 1.6 but previously it was directly executing on the Spark Core engine and whatever optimization needs to be done you have to take care explicitly and you need to understand that how the DataFrame would be converted into RDD and your program as Direct Acyclic Graph. And you must try to reduce the amount of shuffling etc. and filtering out the data before data shuffling. With the Catalyst Optimizer you don't have to worry too much about the optimization. Catalyst optimizer is the heart of SparkSQL, whether you are using Python, Scala, Java, or R language to run SparkSQL code using either SQL queries, DataFrame API or DataFrame Lambda functions all are processed by Catalyst optimizer. Optimizer go through four phases before submitted code is getting executed. Even while going through four phases, it makes sure your code runs fast and optimally distributed on cluster.

To do the optimization Catalyst uses various Scala features like Scala pattern matching, quasiquotes etc. which is based on functional programming construct of Scala.

Objectives of Catalyst optimizer

1. **Optimization technique:** Adding new optimization techniques to the catalyst's optimizer or to SparkSQL module should not be complicated process and must be easy.
2. **Extending Optimizer**: As a user or developer you should be able to add new rules which are specific to your data, as well as support for new data types can be added by you.
   a. **Data specific rules:** By which you should be able to push filtering or aggregations into newer external storage which are not already supported. Many common ones are already supported by SparkSQL itself e.g. JDBC sources Oracle, MySQL etc.
   b. **You** define your own custom data types than you should be able to

create Encoders (serialization and de-serialization : Learn from training) for these newer data types.

Optimization techniques: Catalyst optimizer supports two types of optimization techniques in various phased as below

1. Rule based optimization
2. Cost based optimization

Catalyst Library: **Catalyst framework has its own library and many of the objects, features, API you can use to extend the framework.**

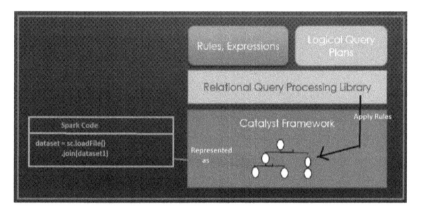

Spark SQL Catalyst Framework

Four phases of Catalyst optimization: **Catalyst optimization has four phases as below.**

1. **Analysis Phase**: Analyzing logical plan and resolve the references by applying rules.
2. **Logical phase**: Optimizing logical plan by applying rules.
3. **Physical planning**: From logical plans create one or more than one physical plan and out of which one will be selected based on lowest cost (cost will be calculated based on CPU, Network I/O and Memory)
4. **Code generation**: generate bytecode to be run on the JVM.

Project Tungsten

Project Tungsten was developed to leverage the modern hardware capability and core focus was on memory and CPU usage by Spark. As you know day by day CPU are also improving and capacity of L1/L2/L3 cache of the CPU is increasing.

Let's assume it if you are working with the 250 nodes of Spark Cluster than how much overall CPU cache is available to you. Assuming each node has 8 core CPU than in total 250X8=2000 Cores are available. Each core can have 256KB CPU cache (L1/L2/L3) than total cache volume is available to you is 500MB which is ultra-fast, because it is attached to your CPU and help you to store your most frequently used data as well as during sorting and hashing it can be used. Hence, this is one of the examples how this Project Tungsten is focusing and leveraging modern hardware for achieving high performant compute cluster.

Even Spark by-passes the in-built features of garbage collection mechanism of java to improve the computation performance.

Following four were the main area of focus for Project Tungsten

1. Explicit Memory Management
2. Binary Data Processing
3. Cache aware computation
4. Code Generation for expressions

We will discuss each one in detail in next section.

Therefore, there are mainly three areas of improvements.

1. Network I/O and Disk I/O
2. In memory (RAM) storage
3. Leveraging CPU caches

Spark team had proved that improving on Disk and Network I/O overall gives 20% performance improvements but if you need more performance than you have to leverage the modern CPU caches as well and push the calculations as close to hardware as possible using L1/L2/L3 caches. As part of Project Tungsten entire focus was optimizing RAM and CPU cycles. Let's see each optimization technique one by one with little more detail.

Explicit Memory Management

As you know Spark framework code is written using Scala and Scala code compiles to Java Bytecode and then finally run in JVM (Java Virtual Machine). JVM gives a lot of features to manage the object lifecycle from creation to destroy as well as platform independence etc. For general purpose applications and even all the enterprise application it is good to rely on this JVM features. Because lot of things which you will be doing like in C language allocation and de-allocation of memory is taken care by the JVM itself and even JVM default object life cycle management is also good enough for almost all enterprise and general-purpose applications. Until and unless you need ultra-high-speed computing like Spark computations on big data, low latency trading etc. For some extent you can optimize the Garbage collection algorithms of Java as well and that may be good enough for your application.

Let's see some basics of Java Garbage Collection mechanism in general

Eden	Survivor-0	Survivor-1	Young	Old

Java Object Garbage Collection Phases

As you can see in the above diagram, when you create an object it is first placed in the Eden space and whenever GC runs and if the object does not have references, it would be destroyed. But if still has references it would be moved to "Survivor-0" space. And same algorithm is applied, if object is still surviving it will be moved to the "Survivor-1" and at the end object will reach in the Old space. Hence, if object is retained for longer time and even on GC runs on space not frequently as it is done on Eden space. Which causes the object remain in the Old generation even if it does not have references. This is what happens in general with the GC algorithm.

DataFrame API

This is one of the most developer friendly changes which are done as part of Spark 2.x release. Previously developer has to use RDD API (this is the core of Spark Framework, still your entire DataFrame code would be converted into RDD and DAG) but before that lot of optimization done to execute your program or instructions as much fast as possible.

DataFrame

Similar to RDD, it is also distributed and immutable collections of data. You can imagine DataFrame as an RDBMS table with column name and rows. But DataFrame rows are divided and saved across various machines in Spark cluster as shown in below image.

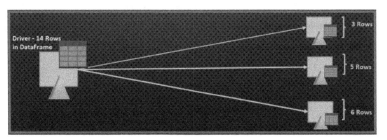

Partitioned DataFrame object across cluster nodes

- DataFrame helps in writing SparkSQL code using simpler API, and it is very similar to Python and R DataFrame.
- DataFrame is higher level abstraction of RDD.

Whenever you work with DataFrame you are working with the Row objects

Even, you can apply schema information to DataFrame object as well. To work with DataFrame you have following two approaches.

- SQL queries
- Query DSL (It can check the syntax at compile time)

DataFrame API makes life easier for the developer. As we move ahead, we will discuss more about all this stuff, while discussing each topic related to CRT020 certification syllabus. There are too much to write about Spark SQL and DataFrame API. In this book our focus is certification preparation so will not go in further depth.

Chpater-4: Spark Architecture Components

About CRT020 Certification Syllabus

If you check the syllabus it is quite huge and you should have a good amount of fundamental concepts cleared and well-practiced all the questions given here. In total there are 10 sections which are being evaluated in the exam and each section could have around 4 to 6 topics. Which makes entire syllabus to cover 40+ topics. Which is quite a huge syllabus compare to any other certifications. The advantage of this, once you learn all the concepts mentioned in the certification, you would become expert in Spark framework. We will go through each topic mentioned in the syllabus one by one and try clear all your concepts. We would divide entire syllabus into 10 different chapters correspond to each section.

Driver

In your Spark application you would be having one component that is known as Driver, driver is a program using which you create a SparkContext object which is connected to the Spark master which can be a Local, Standalone or YARN etc. Driver program can an independently located or can be placed on the same node where master exists. Driver must be accessible from all the worker nodes as well over the network. You would be having some code written your Spark application as below

```
# IP address of the master or you can provide as
#yarn in case of Hadoop
        conf = SparkConf()
                .setMaster("URL for the Master")
                .setAppName("HESparkApp")

        sc = spark.SparkContext(conf)
```

Driver has the following responsibilities

- Driver code will create the SparkContext (Entry point to the Spark Cluster) and declares all the operations like transformations and actions and create DAG (Direct Acyclic Graph)
- Next, driver would submit the serialized RDD graph to the master. And then its master responsibility to divide entire DAG into smaller tasks and submit them to workers for further executions.
- Worker are nodes in the cluster where all the divided tasks would be executed in parallel on the RDD partitions.

In case of Hadoop master can be "yarn" (Yet another resource negotiator). You would be writing your application main method (this is a starting point of your application). So if you think in terms of Java then this is a Class where you would be writing your public static void main(String args[]) method. It depends on what mode you are using

- **Cluster mode**: In case of cluster mode driver would run on one of the machine/nodes which is part of the cluster itself. For example, in case of YARN, driver runs inside

an application master process which is
managed by YARN on the cluster and client
would go away once the application
initiated.
- **Client mode**: Driver runs in the client process
(part of the same process which initiate your
application)

Command line example for submitting application
using cluster and client mode are below.

```
spark-submit
    --master yarn \
    --deploy-mode cluster \
    --driver-memory 12g \
    --executor-memory 2g \
    --executor-cores 1 \
    --queue nameofthequeue \
    hePySparkApp.py
```

Similarly, for the client mode, you can start spark
shell as below.

```
spark-shell --master yarn --deploy-mode client
```

So, we can say that SparkContext is the coordinator
for the submitted application (which runs under the
Driver process).

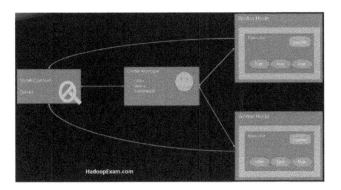

As you can see in above image, once the resources are acquired for running the application tasks, then SparkContext would submit the tasks on the executor. One Spark application is equivalent to having one SparkContext object.

Remember:

- Driver program keep listening for the incoming connections for the executors until the application runs. Driver must be always available on the network.
- You should always run the Drive process near the worker nodes, if possible.
- If you wanted to explicitly assign the memory for driver process in your application then you have to use it like this "spark-submit –driver-memory 4g"
- Your entire application state is maintained in the Driver process.

- Driver process connects with the Cluster manager to get the resources from the Cluster, once it gets the physical resources from cluster. Same would be used to launch the executors.
- Driver also stores the metadata about the currently running application and same application you can see in the web UI.

Executor

- Each application has its own executor processes and remain up only until your application and tasks runs. And make sure your application runs isolated and does not interact with any other application already submitted. Tasks created for each application runs in a different JVM.
- Data between the running application cannot be shared directly.
- If you want to share the data between the running application then first that data needs to be stored on the external storage and then only application can share the data.
- All the tasks which needs to be executed on the executor are assigned by the driver.
- Executor would run the tasks and report back their state and result to the driver.

- Executor tries to store applications data in memory, if there is not enough memory then it will store the same on the Disk.

Cores/Slots/Threads

In Spark Core or Slots represent number of threads available to each executor process. As you can see in the below image

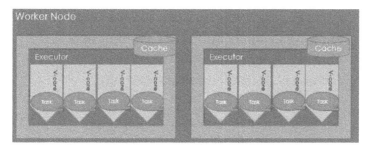

There are 4 cores available to each executor on the worker node. Hence, there are total 8 cores on this given worker node which can execute at the max 8 tasks in parallel. Each individual core at the max can have single thread running. You can use these terms core, thread and slot interchangeably, only for Spark.

Partitions

Let's understand things conceptually at first. If you have huge volume of data which may not fit on a single machine then you split them in multiple parts. For example, you have a Data size of 5TB and your computer has the capacity of 1 TB then you need to divide them into 5 parts (1 TB for each machine). Also, you need to sort this 5 TB data, then you would be sorting independently on each machine in parallel. This each one TB data you can consider as a partition, so we can say there are in total 5 partitions.

In case of Apache Spark size is not the reason to partition the data but rather you want to parallelize the work, so that your application runs fast enough. Even Spark keeps the data in the memory of each node, similar thing is depicted in the below block diagram. Where each node has 1 partition from the huge data file. And can be worked upon parallelly.

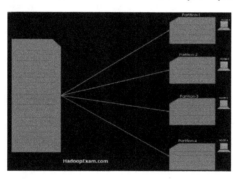

In Spark cluster

- As a developer you can decide how many partitions should be created and also configurable.

- If number of partitions is very few then concurrent computations is also affected and you would have higher latency for your job. And cluster resources not properly utilized.
- Number of partitions you should decide based on the number of cores in your entire cluster. Because at a time a single can work on only one partitions.
- Suppose your cluster has 100 cores then at the max you could have 100 tasks running concurrently in the cluster. So, if you have more than 100 let's say 150 partitions then 50 partitions have to wait for the cores to get free.
- A single RDD partition cannot span more than one node.
- All the tuples in the same partitions are guaranteed to be on the same machine.

Partitions Strategy: There are two partition strategy which are popular

- Hash partitioning
- Range Partitioning

Which partition strategy is best fit decided based on the following factor

- Number of cores
- Size of the file

Syllabus Topic-2: Spark's execution model and the breakdown between the different elements

- Jobs
- Tasks
- Stages

Let's learn few terminologies related to the Spark Architectural components.

- **Application**: Your entire program you write using Spark either in Python, Scala, Java or R. Would be called an application (single application). Your one application would have one SparkContext (means one Driver process) and many executors in the cluster.

Below diagram represent one single Spark application.

You would be bundling your entire application is one JAR file (in case of Scala) or create a Python file. While bundling JAR's keep in mind you should not include Hadoop and Spark libraries, because those would be already bundled by the runtime env.

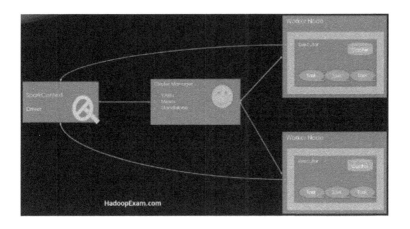

- **Driver**: This is where your main () method would be executed and SparkContext would be created. You can consider Driver as a master for your Spark Application. It also hosts the Web UI for your application. Similarly, tasks schedulers reside on the Driver which schedule tasks that needs to be executed on executors. If your Spark Application got crashed then your Spark application would also be killed.

- **Cluster Manager:** This is the component which is responsible for managing the resources in the entire cluster example YARN, Mesos or Spark Standalone cluster manager. This is used to make sure that no application starves because lack of cluster resource availability.
- **Deployment Modes:** This is not a component but the strategy where your Driver program should run, in case of cluster mode driver process would run on one of the nodes in the cluster and in case of client mode driver process would run outside the cluster.
- **Worker Nodes:** These are the nodes in your cluster which would be running executor process for your application and finally task would be executed on the executor process.
- **Executor**: This is a process which is launched on the Worker Nodes and runs the tasks for your submitted applications and other than this it also keeps the data in memory or disk storage. Each application has its own executors.

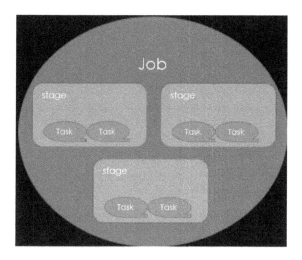

- **Task:** This is the smallest unit of work from your application which would be send to executor specific to an application. Individual tasks run the computation on the a single RDD partitions, as we have multiple partitions of an RDD in a cluster. So various same tasks run on the different partitions of the RDD in the cluster.

A task would always be part of the single stage and work on the single partitions only. Before initiating new stage all the tasks in a stage should be completed. You can also say that task is a command which would be sent from the driver to the executor by serializing the Function object. And executor de-sterilizes this and execute it.

- **Job**: A Job can have multiple tasks (usually it has) which gets Spawned when Spark action is initiated (e.g. collect, count, show etc.). This is very important to remember that Job would be created only when action is executed. Whenever a job is executed, an execution plan is created according to the lineage graph.
    o So, whenever you think about the job, first think how many actions are there in your Spark application.
    o It may be running jobs concurrently.

- **Stages**: A job is sliced into stages, and a stage is a parallel task (one task per partitions), Spark job is sliced into the stages, stage can run on the partitions of the single RDD. For each shuffle new stage would be created. Shuffle introduce a barrier where stages/tasks has to wait previous stage to be finished. It means in a single stage you would not have shuffle. Again, we can say that stage is a collection of tasks, same process runs against different subset of data which is represented as partition. In each stage number of tasks= number of partitions in that stage.

Each stage can be executed on multiple executors and single executor can run multiple v-cores. Each v-core can execute exactly one tasks at a time.

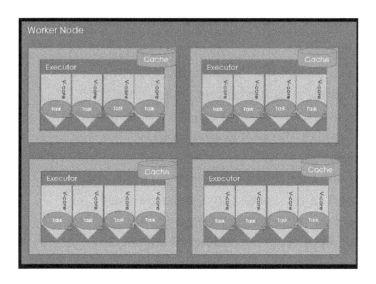

Let's see the below Spark example conceptually to understand more all these terms
- **Step-1**: You would be loading two data files (HECourse.csv and HELearner.csv) as two separate DataFrames
- **Step-2**: Independently replace empty values with Nan in both the DataFrame

- **Step-3**: Join both the DataFrame using the common column.
- **Step-4**: Apply another map function on the data and filter all the Learners where is less than 5000
- **Step-5**: Finally save the DataFrame as Parquet file in HDFS

In above case lets go step by step to understand the stages

- In Step-1 Each file loaded independently, hence there would be two stages created.
- Next stage would be created when shuffle is introduced and that is when join is initialized.
- And all other follow-up operations can also be part of the same stage, because they would be done sequentially and there are no benefits of creating additional stages. So, Saving the data would be part of the same stage. Hence, there would be in total 3 stages.
- How would you calculate total number of tasks in this case?
  Do the sum for all the stages (individual stage X Number of partitions in that stage)

Chapter-6: Spark Concepts

Download Source code: Please use the below URL to download the source code

http://hadoopexam.com/books/code/4DatabricksSparkPythonCRT020/SourceCode.zip

---

Access to Certification Preparation Material
I have already purchased this book printed version from open market, I still wanted to get access for the certification preparation material offered by HadoopExam.com, do you provide any discount for the same.

Answer: First of all, thanks for considering the learning material from HadoopExam.com. Yes, we certainly consider your subscription request and you are eligible for discount as well. What you have to do is that, you can send receipt this book purchase and our sales team can offer you 10% discount on the preparation material. Please send an email to hadoopexam@gmail.com or admin@hadoopexam@gmail.com with the purchase detail and your requirement

Caching

Basic concepts for caching the RDD and DataFrame remain same. There are separate methods are provided to cache/persist the same in the API. To cache the RDD we can use the method like below

```
heRDD.cache()
heRDD.persist()
```

Whether this RDD would be cached on the Disk or in memory is decided by the StorageLevel. If we wanted to know the what storage level is being used by the RDD, we can use the following method

```
heRDD.getStorageLevel
```

Caching is one of the best strategies for boosting the performance in your Spark Application, however we need not to unnecessarily cache/persist the data. Because memory is very critical resource and should not be wasted. Above strategy is known as explicit caching of the data. (Recently Spark announced an availability of automatic caching of the hot data for the user and load balance the cluster: which is part of Databricks solution).

You should use this explicit caching for the storing the results of an arbitrary computation e.g. input or intermediate results, and this can be re-used multiple times. There are some issues as well for explicit caching.

- It requires memory (critical resource and can be used some other purpose) e.g. shuffling and hashing.
- If data is cached on the disk then it needs to be de-serialized again while reading back and make the process slow and sometime this causes performance regression as well.
- It is sometime difficult to find which data needs to be cached and which not generally in interactive application to generate the reports.
- Data engineer can efficiently tune the caching but for the data scientists this is a challenging task.

DataFrame and Caching

As you know, if we want to use the transformation output in later step of calculations, then you cache an RDD, which saves time in future steps. Similarly, DataFrame can be cached. But again, Dataframe are more efficient than RDD, DataFrame will take lesser space compare to RDD to store the same amount of data why? Because Dataframe already know the types of each elements/attributes and take advantage of this. So that while caching them optimally layout the

DataFrame and save the memory space. Even, Dataframe has Encoders which helps in further reducing the space consumed by DataFrame by providing detailed information of the JVM objects.

SparkSQL and Caching

We can cache the RDD in Core Spark, similarly in SparkSQL DataFrame can be cached. Caching will give advantages only when DataFrame are used more than once in an application. If there is no re-use of DataFrame then it is wastage of memory. So, it is always better to un-persist the DataFrame, if it is not used further (Timely un-persisting is an optimization technique in SparkSQL).

dataframe.unpersist() *#un-persisting a dataframe*

Sometime you see when you try to cache a DataFrame, your application may crash. Reason, what type of caching you have configured and size of Dataframe. Suppose size of the DataFrame is quite bigger and not enough memory is available than application will crash. And also caching parameters configured one is *"MEMORY_ONLY"*. Change this configuration to *"MEMORY_AND_DISK"*. By doing this you are able to persist bigger DataFrame as well, even memory space is limited. Because with this configuration, whatever data which does not fit in memory will be saved.

Checkpointing in SparkSQL

This is different than caching, still it helps in freezing the contents or saving the contents so that if saved contents needs to be used in future it will be highly performant. Benefits of the checkpointing are

- Logical plan will be truncated.
- It is highly beneficial for iterative programming like machine learning algorithms, where algorithms need to be executed again and again on the same data. It will also good for truncating the logical plan, because in machine learning algorithms logical plan grows almost exponentially.
- Data will be materialized and finally saved on the disk. It is always advisable that you use the file system where data loss will be avoided like HDFS.

Types of Checkpoints

There are two types of checkpoints

1. Eager checkpointing: In this case as soon as checkpoint is reached it will truncate the lineage and start new lineage after checkpointing.

Creating checkpoint after transformations

o If DataFrame size is huge than it will take some time to save the DataFrame over the disk. All the DataFrame which are partitioned across the nodes and saved. Because of data size, performance can be impacted when first time it is saved. Until entire data is saved to checkpoint directory no further steps will be executed.

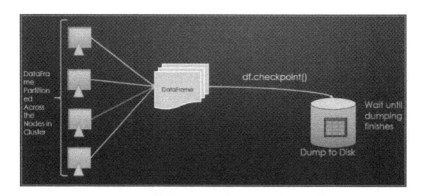

DataFrame checkpoint

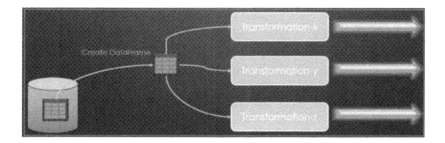

Create DataFrame from Check pointed Data

2. Non-eager/lazy checkpointing: **In this case lineage will not be cut, even after creating the data checkpoint, it will still use the previous lineage.**

Local checkpointing: In this case data will be saved locally on each executor locally.

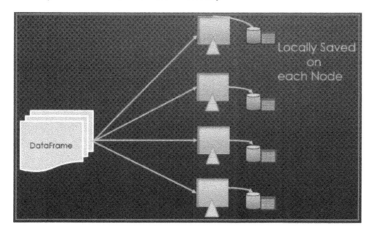

DataFrame Saved locally on each node

Local checkpoints are stored in the executors using caching subsystem and they are not reliable.

Caching (disk only) v/s checkpointing: **What is the difference between caching (disk only) and checkpointing.**

- *DataFrame.persist(disk only)*
- *DataFrame.checkpoint(Eager only)*

DataFrame.persist will serialize the data and keep the data either in cache(memory) or disk. In this case it will remember the lineage. If DataFrame is lost even from disk or memory than it can be created using lineage.

However, eager checkpoint will not store the lineage but rather cut the lineage and data will be persisted on the disk. New DataFrame will be created from the Data store in checkpoint directory. And any new transformation after checkpoint will start a new lineage. In case any node crashes after checkpoint creation it will start lineage from the point where last checkpoint was created by loading data from checkpoint dir.

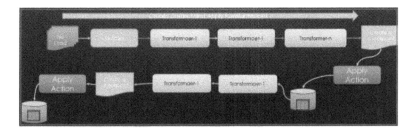

Lineage will cut as soon as action called

Performance Improvements

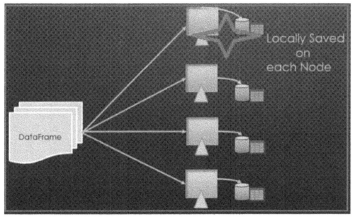

Node crash with the DataFrame Partition

If we don't use caching or checkpointing than Spark will have to re-compute the entire lineage in case of loss of any data on any node, as shown in above image and this will result in huge performance issue.

- **Checkpointing is more reliable**: If you are working with the larger DataFrame and computation is quite complex then checkpointing will be better. Because after doing complex computation data will be stored on the disk and also cut the lineage. However, checkpointing will be slower for the larger DataFrame.

Other important points about checkpointing
- It is good for iterative algorithm like Machine Learning, where lineage can grow exponentially.
- Checkpointing will cut the lineage of underline RDD (Because it is a feature of RDD)
- Eager: It would be done immediately.
- Lazy: Done only when action is executed.
- Checkpoint Directory: Checkpoint will store data in a directory. Hence, it is mandatory that you have already set the checkpoint dir as below

SparkContext.setCheckPointDir()

- If checkpoint dir is not set and you call the checkpoint method on DataFrame, it will give error.

Caching is lazy: If you are doing caching/persist method call on the DataFrame/RDD/DataFrame then remember this is a lazy operation. And

DataFrame would not be cached until an Action is called.

Cache v/s Persist: Calling cache on DataFrame is same as calling persist(MEMORY_ONLY). Because calling cache means saving data in-memory. And using persist method you can use disk as well for caching the data.

- **MEMORY_AND_DISK**: In this case if data does not fit in memory then it would be cached on the disk.
- **MEMORY_ONLY_SER**: In this case DataFrame would be saved on the Disk as serialized Java objects. This is CPU intensive (serialization and deserialization are involved) but save memory. In this case it is possible that some partitions may not be cached and on need basis they are calculated on the fly.
- **MEMORY_ONLY_DISK_SER**: Same as above, but also uses Disk when memory is not enough.
- **DISK_ONLY**: Entire data would be stored on the disk.

Sample code for caching DataFrame

```
#Cache the DataFrame( MEMORY_AND_DISK)
heCourseDF.cache()
```

Shuffling

As name suggest shuffle is the process to re-distribute the data across the nodes or on the same node based on the partition strategy. This process is also known as re-partitioning. Always comes in mind that shuffling happens only among the nodes, but no this is not true. Shuffling is the process of data transfer between stages.

Shuffling is a costly process and we should avoid as much as possible. Shuffling process generally does not reduce the number of partitions but content in a partition are shuffled. Following are some example of the API methods which can cause the shuffle

- *groupByKey*: This shuffle all the data
- *join , cogroup, groupBy* etc.

In shuffle there are two things, shuffle read and shuffle write.

- Shuffle Write: This value represents the sum of all written serialized data on all executors before transmitting usually at the end of a stage.
- Shuffle read: sum of read serialized data on all executors at the beginning of a stage

Suppose you have created an RDD using a collection example below

```
X=heRDD.getNumPartitions()
groupByRDD = heRDD.groupByKey()
Y= groupByRDD.getNumPartitions()
```

Here, X and Y would return the same value. As we discussed it does not change the number of partitions. Now do the similar things with the DataFrame and try to fetch the number of partitions after groupBy transformation

```
heDF.groupBy("key")
heDF.rdd.getNumPartitions()
```

You can observe that number of partitions suddenly increases, which is usually you see 200. Because there is a default configuration value of the parameter *"spark.sql.shuffle.partitions"* is 200. If you don't have enough number of partitions then reduce this value otherwise your jobs would run unnecessarily and cause performance issue.

Partitioning

As we already know that Spark is a Distributed computation engine, where on different data same computation happens on each node in parallel. Part of entire collection of data reside over each node is known as a partition.

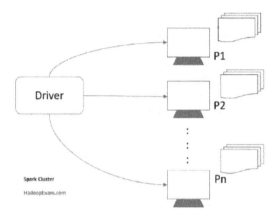

Spark Cluster with DataFrame Partitioning

Data would be partitioned based on the following, to decide what partition strategy to be used:

1. Number of cores in executors
2. Size of the data

Based on above two values, Spark optimizes the parallelism while processing the data. Also, there is a one parameter which decides number of partitions for a DataFrame, which is below.

spark.sql.shuffle.partitions

This parameter is having default value as 200. If you want to change the value in your SparkSession, you can use **spark.conf.set** operator to update this value, similarly other configuration parameters you can change. Here spark is an instance of SparkSession.

If you want to check what all are the partitions are currently available than you have to use below function of the DataFrame.

heDF.rdd.partitions.size()

heDS: It is a DataFrame

As you can see partitioning is done on the RDD and not directly on the DataFrame object. Hence, we are first retrieving underline RDD of the DataFrame and checking what is the total number of partitions exists for this RDD.

Repartitioning: If you want to re-partition the data than you have to use below operator.

heDF.repartition(x) #Here x, is a number value for partitions to be created

About coalesce operator of DataFrame
It is considered as a transformation of a DataFrame.

- This also helps you to re-partition the DataFrame in the given number of partitions.
- Let's see the scenario, what happens If current partitions are more than requested partitions

Current → 5 and Requested → 3 *# It will generate new dataframe with 3 partitions*

Current → 5 and Requested → 6*# It will remain as 5 partitions only*

Example-1: Partitions and coalesce functions

```python
%python
from pyspark.sql import Row

#Create a dataframe with 3 partitions
heDF1 = sc.parallelize([Row(1, "Hadoop", 6000, "Mumbai", 5),Row(2, "Spark", 5000, "Pune", 4),Row(3, "Python", 4000, "Hyderabad", 3)] , 3).toDF()

#Check number of partitions
print(heDF1.rdd.getNumPartitions())

#Repartition the Dataframe in 1
heDFNew1=heDF1.repartition(1)

#Check number of partitions
print(heDFNew1.rdd.getNumPartitions())

#Create a dataframe with 3 partitions
heDF2 = sc.parallelize([Row(1, "Hadoop", 6000, "Mumbai", 5),Row(2, "Spark", 5000, "Pune", 4),Row(3, "Python", 4000, "Hyderabad", 3)] , 3).toDF()
```

```
#Check number of partitions
print(heDF2.rdd.getNumPartitions())

#Repartition the DataFrame in 1
heDFNew2=heDF2.coalesce (1)

#Check number of partitions
print(heDFNew2.rdd.getNumPartitions())

#Repartition the Dataframe in 5
#does it create 5 partitions?
heDFNew3=heDF2.coalesce (5)
#Check number of partitions
print(heDFNew3.rdd.getNumPartitions())
```

Wide vs Narrow Transformations

Spark has mainly two things you need to understand when you do the programming, transformation and actions. Very basic thing you need to understand whether you are using RDD API or DataFrame API, underline data structure (RDD/DataFrame) is immutable (it means you can create new RDD/DataFrame from the existing one, but cannot modify) and this is known as transformation. Below is one of the examples of transformation

```
#Let's create a DataFrame
```

```
heDF = spark.read.format("csv")
.option("header",True)
.option( "Inferschema", True)
.load("HadooExam_Training.csv")

#Using filter function
filteredDF = heDF.filter(heDF.fee>6000)
```

heDF is the DataFrame created from the external source of the data. Now you cannot modify that heDF itself. You have to have create new DataFrame to filter out all the records which are having fee more than 6000. filteredDF is a new DataFrame created after transforming heDF (same DataFrame is not transformed, but new one is created).

Transformations are lazy, they would be evaluated only it founds the actions. Most of the time your code would have lot of transformation, which represent business logic in your Data pipeline or ETL jobs and few of the actions.

There are mainly two types of transformations which you need to understand

- Narrow
- Wide

Let's discuss and understand both of this

At the end all your DataFrame code is also converted to RDD and lineage graph which is also represented as DAG on the RDD.

Narrow transformation: This is also known as transformation with the narrow dependencies. You must know the partition concepts as well to understand this one. Each partition from the input DataFrame/RDD/DataFrame would involve itself with the one output partitions. Suppose your input DataFrame is represented by 5 partitions and after transformation also it would have 5 partitions then this is known as narrow transformation. Below code example represent narrow transformations, by applying filter/where condition would work on the same partitions and no interaction happens between the partitions while applying filter and where condition. You can see in the below image, how it can be represented.

#Using filter function
filteredDF = heDF.filter(heDf.fee>6000)

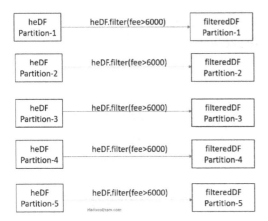

You may get confused that in case of narrow transformation number of partitions should be reduced that is not the case. Narrow transformation does not involve the shuffling as such and does not impact the performance. Below are few examples of transformation which can be possibly narrow

- filter
- flatMap
- mapValues
- mapPartitions etc.

Pipelining with filters: If multiple filters are applied on the DataFrame as below

filteredDF = heDF.filter(fee>6000)
        .filter(name="Spark")

.filter(location="Mumbai")

In this case all the filter operations are applied in memory and represent the narrow transformations. This is an example of pipelining.

Wide transformation: In this case if your input number of partitions are "n" then after applying transformation there would be more than "n" partitions. This happens wherever shuffle (new partitions are created, by exchanging the data between executors, may be across the machines or on the same machine) is involved. Whenever shuffle is applied intermediate data would be written in-memory or on the disk. Example of the transformation which leads to wide transformations are *groupByKey()* and *reduceByKey()*

Shuffle can occur when the next step resultant RDD is depend on the elements from the another RDD.

You can be asked questions based on this, code program would be given and you need to find whether it's a narrow or wide transformation. Please practice all the questions provided by HadoopExam.com

Example of wide transformations (which can have shuffle) are below

- groupByKey
- reduceByKey
- Joins (left,right etc.)
- distinct
- intersection, repartition, coalesce etc.

Join is not always having wide dependencies it can be narrow as well, if data that needs to be joined co-partitioned and does not require shuffling. You can use ". toDebugString" to find out whether shuffling is involved or not.

wordCountRDD = heRDD.map(lambda word : (word,1))
.groupByKey
.toDebugString

Similarly, during runtime if one of the partitions is lost and that needs to be re-computed. If there is narrow transformation then rec-computation would be faster else in case of wide dependency it would be slow. Below block diagram shows the wide transformation for join operation where input data is not co-partitioned.

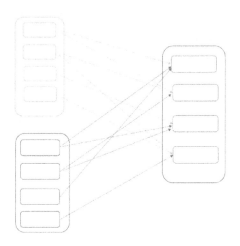

DataFrame Transformations vs Actions vs Operations

Transformation & Actions: As we have discussed above about the transformation, transformation is used by the Spark Framework to create logical plan in the catalyst optimizer. However, to execute the entire DAG of the transformation an action is required. In below example code

hadoopexamLines = lines.filter(contains("HadoopExam"))

both filter and contains method represent the transformation and submitting this code does not do anything and not even trigger any computation. If you want to initiate the computation you have to have action as below.

hadoopexamLines.count()

As soon as Spark find the action, it would trigger the computation and start the execution of DAG. Above action would tell you the number of the records in "hadooexamLines" DataFrame. In above example we have used filter and contains method which does not require any data shuffling. Hence, this is an example of narrow transformations.

Types of actions: There are various different type of actions

- Saving data on filesystem, Database or any supported system example

  hadoopexamLines.saveAsTextFile("hdpcd/hadoopexam6Solved")

- Using action, you can view the data on the console

  hadoopexamLines.show()

- Collecting data in native programming language objects

  hadoopexamLines.collect()

If you wanted to check all the stages, jobs, actions, shuffles, caching etc. then use the Spark Web UI, we have explained the same in detail with our SparkSQL Hands-on Training on HadoopExam.com

Is sorting a wide transformation or narrow?

Answer: As you know to sort the data, it requires data to be shuffled between DataFrame. Hence, this is a wide transformation.

High Level Cluster Configurations

As in your real certification exam you don't have to setup any Spark cluster but they may ask your understanding about how you can change the configuration for your specific application before submitting to cluster etc. (If you find something different in your real exam then please provide feedback at admin@hadoopexam.com)

There are following ways by which we can control the applications

1. **Spark properties**: This can be used to control the application parameters and this can be set using the SparkConf object.
2. **Environment variable**: This is required and would be set per machine (node) basis. If you want to set the IP address you can do using conf/spark-env.sh
3. Logging: This is to change the log level and that can be done usinglog4j.properties file.

Before, after or during the Spark application deployment we should check that the required

Spark properties are set or not. Even many properties we can set on Application level. There are various types of properties which we can set as below.

- Application level
  spark.app.name: Defining the name of the application which can be seen in the log and UI.
  spark.driver.memory: Driver process memory

- Runtime Environment property:
  spark.executor.extraJavaOptions: You can provide additional JVM properties e.g. GC settings.
- Shuffle behavior: These all properties can be used to be applied some changes during the shuffle phase e.g.
  spark.shuffle.compress : Using this you can specify whether the compress the map output or not. If yes then you have to specify the codec as well using below property
  spark.io.compression.codec

There are various such properties which can be specified, hence please know how to set all these properties because we cannot remember all the properties and for that we may have to go through the documentation as well. Below are the different sections for which properties can be defined.

- o Compression and Serialization
- o Memory management
- o Execution behaviour
- o Networking
- o Scheduling
- o Dynamic allocation
- o Security etc.

However, you would be given a particular property detail and you need to find the valid property name and use the same. You can set the Spark properties at below location

- **SparkConf**: Whatever property you set using the SparkConf it would be applied to an individual application parameter. Same properties can be configured using java system properties.
- **Environment variable**: These are machine/node level properties and can be set using conf/spark-env.sh file.
- **Logs level and log rollover settings**: Spark uses the Apache Spark log4J library and individual property can be set using *log4j.properties* file.

Below are some examples for each one of above.

Using *SparkConf* to set properties on the application level

conf = SparkConf().setMaster("yarn").setAppName("HEApp")

sc = SparkContext(conf=conf)

Similarly, dynamically loading Spark properties: This is good way if you want to avoid hardcoding and do the certain configuration in a *SparkConf*. Suppose you want to run your application with different master, you can do as below.

sc = SparkContext(SparkConf())

You would be writing above line in your application and use the below application to submit the code.

spark-submit
> *-- name "HE App"*
> *-- master yarn*
> *-- conf spark.eventLog.enable=false*
> *-- conf "spark.executor.extraJavaOption=-XX:+PrintGCDetails" HEApp.py*

In spark-shell and spark-submit below are the two ways in which properties can be set

- Command line option e.g. *--master*

- Using Configuration object
  --conf

There are some default properties as well, which are set using *conf/spark-default.conf* file. In this file properties can be specified using key and value.

Chapter-7: DataFrames API

Download Source Code

http://hadoopexam.com/books/code/4DatabricksSparkPytho
nCRT020/SourceCode.zip

In the syllabus they have not given any Specific API, but we re-commend you have good experience with the following DataFrame methods, we have covered these in our practice questions (multiple choice as well as assessment, so check here) in Scala and Python both.

DataFrame is mainly represent the Structured API of the Spark which has other components as well like below

- DataFrame (Available in Python and Scala both)
- Creating Temp tables, views etc.

All above are part of syllabus directly or indirectly. This is one of the good training available to learn in detail.

You can even customize the package by selecting your required products and same you can avail on

lesser price for the same contact
admin@hadoopexam.com

DataFrame is a part of Spark SQL module which involves the structure of the data. Let's understand below three components

- RDD (not part of the exam, but core of the Spark framework)
- DataFrame
- DataFrame (Only available in Scala)

SparkSQL Row (Catalyst Row) object (API Doc Link):
It is a generic object in SparkSQL which represent one record in a DataFrame and you can access the fields from Row object using either column name or based on their index position. You can create Row object by providing values like

#Create Row object using values

Row(value1, value2, value3... valuen)

#creating Row object using Seq of values

Row([value1, value2, value3... valuen])

It seems they are very similar to array, and you can access the fields using

1. Index Position
2. Column Name
3. Scala pattern matching

A Row object can have schema as well, but that is not mandatory. Row encoders are responsible for assigning schema to a row. You can access the schema for a Row object using *Row.schema()* method.

Let's see the example with the Row instance.

Example-2: Example to understand Row object

```python
%python
from pyspark.sql import Row

#Import Row object
#Create Rows instances
row = Row("Hadoop" ,5000,"Mumbai" ,400001 )
row1 = Row("Spark" ,5000,"Pune" ,111045 )
row2 = Row("Cassandra" ,5000,"Banglore" ,530068 )

#Accessing values from Row using ordinal position
print(row[0])
print(row[1])
print(row[2])
print(row[3])

#Import types
from pyspark.sql.types import StructType
from pyspark.sql.types import StructField
from pyspark.sql.types import StringType,IntegerType

#Define a course_detail type which can hold upto three
venues
```

```
course_detail = StructType([StructField("name", StringType(),
True)
                    , StructField("Fee", IntegerType(), False)
                    , StructField("City", StringType(), False)
                    , StructField("Zip", IntegerType(), False)  ])
```

#Now create the DataFrame using the schema we have
created above
```
HEDF =
spark.createDataFrame(spark.sparkContext.parallelize([row,
row1, row2]),course_detail)
```

#Check whether valid schema is assigned or not
```
HEDF.printSchema()
```

#Check the data
```
HEDF.show()
HEDF.schema
```

#Print tree format Schema
```
HEDF.printSchema()
```

Resilient Distributed DataFrame

RDD is the lowest representation of data in
Spark. Every processing in Spark done using RDD,
whether you use SparkSQL abstractions like
DataFrame. An RDD spread across multiple
machines in a Spark cluster, it provides APIs so you

can work on it. You can create an RDD from different types of data source, e.g. text files, a database via JDBC, etc.

Apache Definitions of RDD: RDDs are fault-tolerant, parallel data structures that let users explicitly persist intermediate results in memory, control their partitioning to optimize data placement, and manipulate them using a rich set of operators.

To learn RDD API and For Hands On session we recommend this training from Spark Core training on http://HadoopExam.com

DataFrame**:**

Similar to RDD, it is also distributed and immutable collections of data. You can imagine DataFrame as an RDBMS table with column name and rows. But DataFrame rows are divided and saved across various machines in Spark cluster as shown in below image.

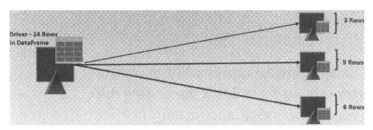

Partitioned DataFrame object across cluster nodes

- DataFrame helps in writing SparkSQL code using simpler API, and it is very similar to Python and R DataFrame.
- DataFrame is higher level abstraction of RDD.

Here Row is a generic object, and does not have type information attached to it.

Whenever you work with DataFrame you are working with the Row objects.

Even, you can apply schema information to DataFrame object as well. To work with DataFrame you have following two approaches.

- SQL queries
- Query DSL (It can check the syntax at compile time)

Programmatically assigning schema:

For creating schema programmatically, we have to use following Spark classes, specific to Schema

- StructType
- StructFields

Where StructType is a sequence of StructFields. It can be done as below

```
heDF =
spark.read.format("csv").schema(customSchemaString).load(
"csv file path").toDF("columnNames String")
```

In above case, whatever column names and StructFields you have provided in custom schema must match. If it does not match than there will be an error.

Example-3: Work with the DataFrame

```python
%python
from pyspark.sql import Row

#Create an RDD with 5 HECourses
courseRDD = sc.parallelize([(1, "Hadoop", 6000, "Mumbai", 5)
                , (2, "Spark", 5000, "Pune", 4)
                , (3, "Python", 4000, "Hyderabad", 3)
                , (4, "Scala", 4000, "Kolkata", 3)
                , (5, "HBase", 7000, "Banglore", 7)])

#Create a DataFrame from RDD
courseRDD.toDF()

#Let's check the data
display(courseRDD.toDF())

#Create a DataFrame with 5 Row objects
spark.createDataFrame([
Row(1, "Hadoop", 6000, "Mumbai", 5)
```

```
,Row(2, "Spark", 5000, "Pune", 4)
,Row(3, "Python", 4000, "Hyderabad", 3)
,Row(4, "Scala", 4000, "Kolkata", 3)
,Row(5, "HBase", 7000, "Bangalore", 7)]).show()
```

```
#Creating DataFrame from csv file
heDF =
spark.read.format("com.databricks.spark.csv").option("heade
r", "true").load("/FileStore/tables/HadooExam_Training.csv")

heDF.printSchema()
display(heDF)
```

In the above example we can see that there are
multiple ways by which we can create DataFrame
like from RDD, from Sequence of Row objects and
loading files etc.

DataFrame is an un-typed or generic collection of
rows. You can convert an RDD to a DataFrame using
a method toDF(), also this is one of the good ways if
you want to re-name the columns in DataFrame, we
will see example in next section.

Question: What do you think about printSchema()
method of DataFrame is an action or
transformation?

Answer: printSchema does not initiate any
computation and no new Job will be launched. All

the schema information stored with the DataFrame will be shown, hence it is a transformation. (It's a common interview question)

DataFrame internally stores the logical plan and represents the computation which is required to produce this DataFrame, as soon as action is triggered on that DataFrame this logical plan will be submitted for optimization by catalyst optimizer and finally one or more than one physical plan will be generated and cost based optimizer will be choosing the best physical plan (you can provide hints as well in some cases, so that catalyst choose the plan based on the hint provided by you). If you use explain (Boolean) method of DataFrame, it will give you the entire detail about the plan which will be used.

DataFrame will always have **Encoders**, if you know the Java serialization and de-serialization then Encoders are the same thing but much more efficient than Java default serialization and de-serialization mechanism. For all the commonly used datatypes like int, float, Boolean etc. encoders are already provided by the SparkSQL. If you are having some custom datatypes than you have to define your own custom Encoders. Let's say we have an object called *HECourse(ID,name,fee)* with three fields, Spark already have defined Encoders for Integer and String, so you do not have to create custom encoders.

With the help of Encoders, Spark at runtime generate binary data for this HECourse instance and even SparkSQL is so smart enough that it will work only on this binary data, without converting back them to original object that gives a lot of performance boost for the Catalyst optimizer. And binary data take much less memory space than actual object. We will be using DataFrameReader to create DataFrame object.

Dataframe

DataFrame is higher level abstraction to work with Apache SparkSQL. Using this API, you can work with structured (e.g. csv) as well as with semi-structured data (JSON). DataFrames are created or represent object in JVM. If any object present in JVM it means it had resolved its reference name as well as its type is known to the system.

Similar to RDD, DataFrame is distributed as well immutable. Hence, if you want to create new DataFrame from existing DataFrame you have to use transformation API, which can help you to get the desired DataFrame from existing DataFrame.

- It is there since Spark 1.6

- More focus was performance, and use of SparkSQL catalyst engine.
- DataFrame is not available in Python and R language Spark API. But same functionality can be achieved using DataFrame because Python is dynamic type of language. And Scala and Java are static type language.
  - In case of DataFrame, if column name are not known in advanced then it will be created using generic column named like ($\_c0, \_c1,....\_cn$)

Working with DataFrame

You can assume DataFrame as a logical plan in a SparkSession, a logical plan describes how all the computations can be applied. We can create DataFrame using

- Files (csv, sequence, Avro, parquets, JSON etc.)
- From Hive tables.
- RDBMS tables.
- NOSQL databases like Cassandra, HBase etc.

Transient: If a variable is transient then it would not be serialized.

To select particular column from the DataFrame, you can use column name or col function of the

DataFrame. SparkSQL revolves around DataFrame, which internally uses Catalyst optimizer. Let's see few examples to work with DataFrame and then slowly we will move further for more API functions.

```python
%python
from pyspark.sql import Row

#Create an RDD with 5 Row
courseRDD = sc.parallelize([
  Row(1, "Hadoop", 6000, "Mumbai", 5)
 , Row(2, "Spark", 5000, "Pune", 4)
 , Row(3, "Python", 4000, "Hyderabad", 3)
 , Row(4, "Scala", 4000, "Kolkata", 3)
 , Row(5, "HBase", 7000, "Banglore", 7)]
)

#Check the types of RDD
print(courseRDD)

#Convert RDD into dataFrame,
#This RDD does not have schema assigned, we need to create one and then assign it
from pyspark.sql.types import StructField, StringType, IntegerType, StructType

data_schema = StructType([StructField('id', IntegerType(), True),StructField('name', StringType(), True),StructField('fee', IntegerType(), True), StructField('venue', StringType(), True),StructField('duration', IntegerType(), True)])
```

```
#Assign the Schema to DataFrame
heCourseDF = courseRDD.toDF(data_schema)
print(heCourseDF)

#Select the courses conducted in Mumbai, having price more
#than 5000
#Also, you can select the columns, you need (It is DSL)
filteredDF = heCourseDF.where("fee
>5000").where("venue=='Mumbai'").select(heCourseDF.name
,heCourseDF.fee, heCourseDF.duration, heCourseDF.venue)

#You can see filteredDF is a DataFrame
print(filteredDF)

#Lets make code more SQL friendly as it is SparkSQL
#Register DataFrame as temporary view and will be added in
#Catalog
filteredDF.createOrReplaceTempView("T_HECOURSE")

#Use SQL Query
filteredSQLDS = sql("SELECT * FROM T_HECOURSE  WHERE
fee > 5000 AND venue = 'Mumbai' ")

#Show the result
filteredSQLDS.show()
```

DataFrame vs RDD operations

If you have already been using RDD for your Spark programming, you will see that working with the SparkSQL for similar operation is much easier that directly working with the RDD.

Other than that, we can conclude that

- Using RDD you cannot run SQL query while with DataFrame you can do
- Using RDD code optimization is your headache and using DataFrame it is taken care by Catalyst optimizer
- Writing transformation code is much more convenient if used with DataFrame than RDD.
- DataFrame uses more efficient Encoders than RDD. Hence, further improvement for the performance.
- You can visualize the data in tabular format, which is not always possible with the RDD. Hence, it makes writing code even friendlier.
- Most of the time you will be writing lesser code while using DataFrame than RDD for doing the same operations.
- DataFrame is highly performant than RDD.

Converting an RDD to DataFrame

You can convert an RDD to DataFrame using toDF method as below

heCourseDF = courseRDD.toDF()

Print the explain plan in all three cases

Example-5: Understanding of the explain plans

%python

from pyspark.sql import Row

#Create an RDD with 5 Row
courseRDD = sc.parallelize([
  Row(1, "Hadoop", 6000, "Mumbai", 5)
  , Row(2, "Spark", 5000, "Pune", 4)
  , Row(3, "Python", 4000, "Hyderabad", 3)
  , Row(4, "Scala", 4000, "Kolkata", 3)
  , Row(5, "HBase", 7000, "Banglore", 7)]
)

#Check the types of RDD
print(courseRDD)

#Convert RDD into dataFrame,
#This RDD does not have schema assigned, we need to create
#one and then assign it
from pyspark.sql.types import StructField, StringType,
IntegerType, StructType

```python
data_schema = StructType([StructField('id', IntegerType(),
True),StructField('name', StringType(), True),StructField('fee',
IntegerType(), True), StructField('venue', StringType(),
True),StructField('duration', IntegerType(), True)])

#Assign the Schema to DataFrame
heCourseDF = courseRDD.toDF(data_schema)
print(heCourseDF)

#Select the courses conducted in Mumbai, having price more
#than 5000
#Also, you can select the columns, you need (It is DSL)
filteredDF = heCourseDF.where("fee
>5000").where("venue=='Mumbai'").select(heCourseDF.name
,heCourseDF.fee, heCourseDF.duration, heCourseDF.venue)

#You can see filteredDF is a DataFrame
print(filteredDF)

#Lets make code more SQL friendly as it is SparkSQL
#Register DataFrame as temporary view and will be added in
#Catalog
filteredDF.createOrReplaceTempView("T_HECOURSE")

#Use SQL Query
filteredSQLDS = sql("SELECT * FROM T_HECOURSE  WHERE
fee > 5000 AND venue = 'Mumbai' ")

#Show the result
filteredSQLDS.show()
```

DataFrame has organized column names in it. There are too many methods which you need to have some practice, we are listing below which are critical to learn.

DataFrame operations: You should have tried this all transformations and actions before your exam and you should be able to find the correct syntax during the exam asap from the given API doc. If you memorize as much as possible then it's very good. (You can check on the HadoopExam.com whether revision notes are available, if yes, use that to memorize the required thing from this)

Chapter-8: SparkContext

Under this subject you would be able to create SparkContext (In spark-shell or pyspark shell it is by default available with the variable name "sc") or SparkSession (available as "spark" variable in shell). You can use HadoopExam.com practice material and videos to understand more how this environment works.

In your application you should use the SparkSession in the driver program which has a handle to the SparkContext object as well. And SparkContext has the access to set the configuration properties via the SparkConf object. SparkConf object stores the configuration parameters for your application as well as some are used by Spark to allocate the resources in the cluster.

SparkContext require an object of SparkConf which has the information about your application. Also, make sure per JVM only one SparkContext object is created. Below is the sample Scala code to create and initialize the Spark application

heConf = SparkConf().setAppName("HadoopExam HDPSCD Spark").setMaster(master)
heSparkContext = SparkContext(conf=heConf)
Where

AppName: Name of your Spark Application, which would be printed in all your logs or on the Web GUI.

master: It could be anything from below

- **Local/spark**: provided by the Spark itself. Local should be used only for testing and unit testing.
- **Mesos**
- **Yarn**: For this certification this is the relevant one and you should always use this one for this

certification. While using the spark-submit command also you have to use this one.

In this exam they would not ask you to use different master modes. Even some stub code already be provided to you. You need to complete the remaining task using that stub code.

With the SparkContext our Spark application get access to the Spark cluster using the ResourceManager. As we have following resource managers available

- Local mode: Using number of threads as local[n]
- SparkStandAlone: Spark Default resource managers.
- Yarn: Hadoop Yet another resource negotiator.
- Mesos

Using SparkContext we can

- Cancel already submitted Job, hence it works as a handle for the submitted application.
- Set the configurations.
- Get the current status of the already submitted applications and few more things

We can still use the SparkContext object, mainly while working with RDD api and shared variables (Broadcast variable and Accumulators)

conf = SparkConf().serMaster(yarn).setAppName("HE App")
sc = new SparkConf(conf=conf)

SparkSession is a unification of various already available context like

- SQLContext
- Sparkcontext
- HiveContext
- StreamingContext

SparkContext should be used if you are using version before Spark 2.x and using the SparkConf() object we can do the various configuration as below

import org.apache.spark.{SparkContext, SparkConf}

```
conf = pyspark.SparkConf()
conf.setAppName("finance-similarity-app")
conf.setMaster('spark:#11.11.11.1:8091')
conf.set('spark.executor.memory', '2g')
conf.set('spark.executor.cores', '4')
conf.set('spark.cores.max', '40')
conf.set('spark.logConf', True)
```

SparkConf once created then its immutable for your application and you should use SparkConf to configure each individual application.

If explicitly not mentioned and you have handle to SparkSession as well then you can use SparkSession object to do the configuration.

However, in the syllabus they have mentioned you should be able to do basic cluster configuration using the SparkContext object. But you can also use the SparkSession to do the same for example as below.

```
spark.conf.set("spark.sql.shuffle.partitions", 6)
spark.conf.set("spark.executor.memory", "2g")
```

Here, spark is an object of SparkSession and SparkSession has a member variable called "conf" which represent the RuntimeConfig object and can be used to do configuration at runtime. As per the API doc this is an interface through which you can get and set all Spark and Hadoop configurations which are relevant to SparkSQL. When getting the value of a config, this defaults to the value set in the underlying SparkContext.

If in the exam Databricks ask you to set any specific configuration properties then you can do as below, if it is related to SparkSQL

To prevent a query from creating too many output rows for the number of input rows, you can enable Query Watchdog and configure the maximum number of output rows as a multiple of the number of input rows. In this example we use a ratio of 1000.

spark.conf.set("spark.databricks.queryWatchdog.enabled", true)

spark.conf.set("spark.databricks.queryWatchdog.outputRatio Threshold", 1000L)

spark.conf.set("spark.databricks.queryWatchdog.maxHivePar titions", 20000)

spark.conf.set("spark.databricks.queryWatchdog.maxQueryT asks", 20000)

This is same as we did before, you just need to find the properties key and value. And use either SparkContext or SparkSession to configure the properties. If it is related to Spark SQL then use the SparkSession object else you can go for SparkContext way. If you are creating SparkSession object yourself then you can also use the below method to set the config properties while create SparkSession object

```
SparkSession.builder
    .master("local")
    .appName("Word Count")
    .config("spark.some.config.option", "some-value")
    .getOrCreate()
```

In general Spark has 3 options to configure the properties

- Using SparkConf object as we have seen above
- You can even use the Java System properties (In exam they would not ask this thing)
- Some properties hard coded in the file (again they would not ask this in exam)

Chpater-9: SparkSession

Download Source code

http://hadoopexam.com/books/code/4DatabricksSparkPytho
nCRT020/SourceCode.zip

SparkSession

This is an entry point for the Spark env. This is available since Spark 2.x version. Since then many things have changed for the Apache Spark. As we have seen before Spark 2.0, entry point was SparkContext

With the SparkContext our Spark application get access to the Spark cluster using the

ResourceManager. As we have following resource managers available

- Local mode: Using number of threads as local[n]
- SparkStandAlone: Spark Default resource managers.
- Yarn : Hadoop Yet another resource negotiator.
- Mesos

Using SparkContext we can

- Cancel already submitted Job, hence it works as a handle for the submitted application.
- Set the configurations.
- Get the current status of the already submitted applications and few more things

We can still use the SparkContext object, mainly while working with RDD api and shared variables (Broadcast variable and Accumulators)

conf = SparkConf().serMaster(yarn).setAppName("HE App")
sc = new SparkConf(conf=conf)

SparkSession is a unification of various already available context like

- SQLContext
- Sparkcontext
- HiveContext
- StreamingContext

We can create SparkSession as below.

```
from pyspark.sql import SparkSession
SparkSession = SparkSession.builder
                    .master("yarn")
                    .appName("HeApp")
                    .config("key", "value")
                    .getOrCreate()
```

We can use SparkSession to read the data.

```
df = SparkSession.read.json("heData.json")
```

There is various format specific method available on SparkSession, which you should have practiced well before your real exam. Below are some of the examples

- *spark.csv()*
- *spark.jdbc()*
- *spark.json()*
- *spark.orc()*
- *spark.parquet()*
- *spark.text()*
- *spark.textFile()*

All above are the format specific methods. If you want to use format agnostic method then use load() method and then you have to use format() method to specify the format of the Data.

Once the data is read then it would return DataFrameReader object.

Create DataFrame from a collection (e.g. list or set)

There are various ways to create DataFrame in the Spark but it all depends on what is the source for creating the DataFrame, whether you are using file, collection or RDBMS etc. We will check all the different ways of creating the DataFrame one by one. As per the syllabus lets first see how we can create DataFrame using the collection, so let's go from below example

Example-6: Creating DataFrame using the List

%python

#import the SparkSession if it is not available
from pyspark.sql import SparkSession
heList = [1,2,3,4,5]

#Create Object of SparkSession
spark = SparkSession.builder.master("local").getOrCreate()

#import the implicit, which allows common collection #into
#DatFrame

```
from pyspark.sql.types import IntegerType

# Create DataFrame using the list of numbers
df = spark.createDataFrame(heList, IntegerType())
df.show()
```

We have seen most of the time Learners try to
convert List to RDD first and then convert them into
DataFrame. Which is not required at all. You can
directly convert your list to DataFrame as above.

**Example-7: Converting a map to DataFrame, if you are
having a map which has key:CourseName and value:Fee.
Below is the example to convert map into DataFrame**

```
%python

#import the SparkSession if it is not available

from  pyspark.sql import SparkSession

#Creart an object of SparkSession

spark = SparkSession.builder.getOrCreate()

#import the implicit, which allows common #Define a Map,
as per the requirement

heMap = {'Hadoop':6000, 'Spark':4000 , 'Java':8000}

#Get all the items from the dictionary/map and specify the
schema

df = spark.createDataFrame(heMap.items(), ["CourseName",
"Fee"])
```

df.show()

Example-8: Converting list of List into a DataFrame

%python

#import the SparkSession if it is not available
from pyspark.sql import SparkSession

heListOfList = [["Hadoop", 6000]
,["Hadoop", 6000]
,["Spark", 6000]
,["Java", 6000]
,["Python", 6000]
*]*

#Then you can convert this tuple into DataFrame as below
spark1=SparkSession.builder.getOrCreate()

print(heListOfList)

#If you do this, it will give error
 # error: value toDf is not a member of List[(Any, Any)]
df=spark.createDataFrame(heListOfList, ["CourseName" ,
"Fee"])
df.show()

Example-9: Creating a list of data into DataFrame

%python

```
#import the required types
from pyspark.sql import SparkSession
from pyspark.sql.types import ArrayType, StructField,
StructType, StringType, IntegerType

# Create a List, which has required data
data = [('Hadoop', 8000, "Mumbai"),
    ('Spark', 12000, "Pune"),
    ('Python', 7000, "NewYork")]

# Define a schema for the dataframe
schema = StructType([
    StructField('CourseName', StringType(), True),
    StructField('CourseFee', IntegerType(), True),
    StructField('Location', StringType(), True)
])

# Convert list to RDD
rdd = spark.sparkContext.parallelize(data)

# Create data frame
df = spark.createDataFrame(rdd,schema)
print(df.schema)
df.show()
```

Spark has introduced encoders in Spark 2.x version
which used to convert Java object into Spark
internal binary format objects. Spark also has inbuilt
encoders and you should not create one your own.

Hence, if you want to create DataFrame using Python collection remember you have to do below 3 things first

```
#import the required types
from pyspark.sql import SparkSession


#Then you can convert this tuple into DataFrame as below
spark1=SparkSession.builder.getOrCreate()


#import the required types
from pyspark.sql import SparkSession
from pyspark.sql.types import ArrayType, StructField,
StructType, StringType, IntegerType


#From List you can create DataFrame using and even you can
provide name of columns at the same time
data = [
    ["Hadoop", 6000],
    ["Spark", 7000],
    ["Scala", 9000]
]
df1 = spark.createDataFrame(data
, ["CourseName", "CourseFee"])


df1.show()
```

Create a DataFrame for a range of numbers

Sometime to create an adhoc DataFrame you can use the range of numbers as well. Let see some example of creating DataFrame using the range of number as this is mentioned explicitly in the syllabus.

Example-11: Create DataFrame using Range of Numbers

%python

#If required import SparkSession object
from pyspark.sql import SparkSession

#Create a DataFrame which has course_id starting from 0 to
#99
df = spark.range(0, 100 , 1).toDF("courseid")
df.show(100)

#Create a DataFrame which has course_id starting from 20 to
#80
heDF2 = spark.range(20, 80 , 1).toDF("courseid")
heDF2.show(100)

#adding values to each row with 1000
heDF2.select(heDF2.courseid + 1000).show()

In Spark DataFrame a column can represent an int, string or any complex type elements as in above case it is an int value. Even it can hold a null value as well. While working with the DataFrame you can select a column from the DataFrame as we did in above example. Even we can remove a column from the DataFrame while applying the transformation and new DataFrame would have dropped that column.

Package for the column, you should remember this

from pyspark.sql.functions import col, column

You can use *col ()* function of the DataFrame to select specific column from the DataFrame.

Access the DataFrameReaders

We can use SparkSession to read the data.

df = SparkSession.read.json("heData.json")

There is various format specific method available on SparkSession, which you should have practiced well before your real exam. Below are some of the examples

```
spark.read.|
            csv
          · format
          · jdbc
          · json
            load
            option
            options
            orc
          · parquet
```

All above are the format specific methods. If you want to use format agnostic method then use load() method.

Once the data is read then it would return DataFrameReader object. You can use SparkSession's read method as well to get access to DataFrameReader as below

```
# Get DataFrameReader using SparkSession
dataFrameReader = sparkSession.read

# Set header option to true to specify that first row in file contains
# name of columns
dataFrameReader.option("header", True)
csvDataFrame = dataFrameReader.csv("hedata.csv");
```

Register User Defined Functions (UDFs)

These types of functions will be applied on each row of DataFrame and also generate a single value.

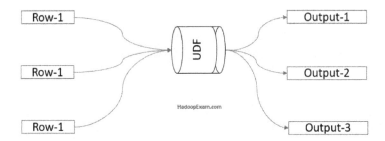

Standard Udf function input and output

UDF: User Defined Functions: You can define some functions for your custom requirement, in case functionality or function is not available in SparkSQL library.

Remember: It is possible that Catalyst may not be able to optimize UDF of your custom requirement. Hence, create UDF only when there is an absolute need.

You can use UDF for both

- DataFrame API
- SparkSQL queries

Following are the ways by which you can define UDF functions

1. Inline UDF creation: Below is an example of defining inline UDF functions

```
#Define a Python function
def heCalculateTotalSalary(s): return s + s*20/100
```

```
#Register the UDF function
spark.udf.register("heCalculateTotalSalary",
heCalculateTotalSalary)
```

In above case function defined is an anonymous function using Lambda features.

2. Explicitly creating function: Below is the pseudo code for creating Scala function and then we can use this function as UDF

```
calculateTotalSalary = udf( _ {

                    -----------------
                    -----------------
                    -----------------
                            }
```

You can use these functions with the DataFrame API, without doing any other step. But if you want to use them in a SQL query than you **have to register this function** using below syntax.

```
spark.udf.register("provideRefrenceName" ,
"functionNameWhichWasDefined")
```

```
spark.udf.register("totalSal" , "calculateTotalSalary")
```

Example-12 for User Defined Function

%python

rowDF= spark.createDataFrame([
Row(1, "Deva", "Male", 5000, "Sales"),
Row(2, "Jugnu", "Female", 6000, "HR"),
Row(3, "Kavita", "Female", 7500, "IT"),
Row(4, "Vikram", "Male", 6500, "Marketing"),
Row(5, "Shabana", "Female", 5500, "Finance"),
Row(6, "Shantilal", "Male", 8000, "Sales"),
Row(7, "Vinod", "Male", 7200, "HR"),
Row(8, "Vimla", "Female", 6600, "IT"),
Row(9, "Jasmin", "Female", 5400, "Marketing"),
Row(10, "Lovely", "Female", 6300, "Finance"),
Row(11, "Mohan", "Male", 5700, "Sales"),
Row(12, "Purvish", "Male", 7000, "HR"),
Row(13, "Jinat", "Female", 7100, "IT"),
Row(14, "Eva", "Female", 6800,"Marketing"),
Row(15, "Jitendra", "Male", 5000, "Finance"),
Row(15, "Rajkumar", "Male", 4500, "Finance"),
Row(15, "Satish", "Male", 4500, "Finance"),
Row(15, "Himmat", "Male", 3500, "Finance")]).toDF("id" ,
"name" , "Gender" , "Salary" , "dept")

rowDF.show()

```
#Define UDF function, which add 20% bonus to salary
#However, remember for SparkSQL, it is difficult to optimize
#UDF functions.
#Hence, you should use as less as possible.
def heCalculateTotalSalary(s): return s + s*20/100

#Register the UDF function
spark.udf.register("heCalculateTotalSalary",
heCalculateTotalSalary)

#Use this UDF function to get total salary
rowDF.withColumn("TotalSalary",
heCalculateTotalSalary(rowDF.Salary)).show()

#Check your function is registered or not
l = spark.catalog.listFunctions()
print(l)
```

Chapter-10: DataFrameReader

Download Source code

http://hadoopexam.com/books/code/4DatabricksSparkPytho
nCRT020/SourceCode.zip

Access to Certification Preparation Material
I have already purchased this book printed version from
open market, I still wanted to get access for the

certification preparation material offered by
HadoopExam.com, do you provide any discount for the
same.
Answer: First of all, thanks for considering the learning
material from HadoopExam.com. Yes, we certainly
consider your subscription request and you are eligible for
discount as well. What you have to do is that, you can send
receipt this book purchase and our sales team can offer
you 10% discount on the preparation material. Please send
an email to hadoopexam@gmail.com or
admin@hadoopexam@gmail.com with the purchase detail
and your requirement

DataFrameReader **(API Doc Link):** It is a class used
to load the data in Spark from external systems like
HDFS, local file system, JDBC store or supported
NoSQL systems. To get the instance of
DataFrameReader we have to use SparkSession
object.
SparkSession.read()

DataFrameReader provides various methods to
read the data from respective external systems like
reading csv, jdbc, json, orc, parquet, exiting spark
sql tables and text files. All the API methods of
DatFrameReader return DataFrame object.

format(source): Specifies the input data source
format.

df = spark.read.format('json').load('heData.json')

Jdbc : Construct a DataFrame representing the database table named table accessible via JDBC URL url and connection properties.

Json: Loads JSON files and returns the results as a DataFrame
　　　df1 = spark.read.json('he_data.json')

load: Loads data from a data source and returns it as a: class`DataFrame`
df = spark.read.format("parquet").load('parquet_partitioned', opt1=True, opt2=1, opt3='str')

df = spark.read.format('json').load(['hedata1.json', 'hedata2.json'])

option(*key, value*) : Adds an input option for the underlying data source

orc(*path*): Loads ORC files, returning the result as a DataFrame.
df = spark.read.orc('heData.orc')

parquet: Loads Parquet files, returning the result as a DataFrame.
You can set the following Parquet-specific option(s) for reading Parquet files:

- **mergeSchema**: sets whether we should merge schemas collected from all Parquet part-files. This will override spark.sql.parquet.mergeSchema. The default value is specified in spark.sql.parquet.mergeSchema

df = spark.read.parquet('heData.parquet')

- **schema**: Specifies the input schema.

s = spark.read.schema("col0 INT, col1 DOUBLE")

table : Returns the specified table as a DataFrame.
df = spark.read.parquet('heData.parquet')
df.createOrReplaceTempView('tmpTable')
spark.read.table('tmpTable')

text: Loads text files and returns a DataFrame whose schema starts with a string column named "value", and followed by partitioned columns if there are any. Each line in the text file is a new row in the resulting DataFrame.

df = spark.read.text('heData.txt')
df = spark.read.text('heData.txt', wholetext=True)
- **wholetext** – if true, read each file from input path(s) as a single row.

If you see above API methods to load the external data, then you will find that there are two types of functions, one which are format agnostic e.g. load(String path) method and other one is format specific like csv(String path)

If you are using format agnostic load method than you have to specify format explicitly using format method of the DataFrameReader. We will see few of the examples of both the variations in next steps.

All the methods return DataFrame, so we can use any of the following ways to do operations.
1. Python Lambda expressions
2. Python Dataframe API
3. SQL Query language by converting DataFrame in either temp or global views.

Read data for the "Core" data formats like CSV, JSON, JDBC, ORC, Parquet, Text and tables

Example-13: DataFrameReader example

%python

#format agnostic load method
#Loading csv file

```
spark.read.format("csv").option("header",True).option("infer
Schema",True).load("/FileStore/tables/HadooExam_Training.
csv").show()

#Loading json file
#You can specify like json, csv, parquet, orc, text, jdbc etc.
spark.read.format("json").option("header",True).option("infe
rSchema",True).load("/FileStore/tables/he_data_1.json").sho
w()

#format specific methods (Will be loaded as DataFrame)
spark.read.json("/FileStore/tables/he_data_1.json").show()
spark.read.json("/FileStore/tables/he_data_1.json").printSch
ema()

#Read csv data
spark.read.csv("/FileStore/tables/HadooExam_Training.csv").
show()
spark.read.csv("/FileStore/tables/HadooExam_Training.csv").
printSchema()

#Reading as textFile, this is the function which returns
DataFrame object
spark.read.text("/FileStore/tables/HadooExam_Training.csv")
.show()

#Split the text
from pyspark.sql.functions import split
df =
spark.read.text("/FileStore/tables/HadooExam_Training.csv")
```

df.withColumn('value',split('value',',')).show()

As we have seen most of the functions return DataFrame object.

Reading Parquet file: You might get many questions which ask you to read already saved parquet data and write or save your DataFrame in a parquet format as below.

Parquet is a columnar file format, which is very frequently used in the BigData world and considered as a highly structured data, because schema is in-built with the Data. Also, one of the most optimized file formats for querying the data. Even much faster than JSON and CSV file format. Below is an example to read and write data I Parquet format.

Example-14: Reading parquet file (We would be using the Same DataFrame which was created in previous example)

df.write.mode("overwrite").parquet("/tmp/testParquet")

#Reading back the stored file using format specific parquet method

data = spark.read.parquet("/tmp/testParquet")

display(data)

ORC File format

ORC is an Optimized Row columnar Data format, mostly we have seen this is used with the Hive. And Spark sometime needs to read data stored directly from the managed storage on Hadoop from where Hive loads the data. It has schema in-built, hence also known as self-describing format another advantage is that it has type information also available which is very good for the catalyst optimizer. However, parquet is more optimized then ORC, which was built after that. Previously, there was no format specific method was available to read the ORC file, but now it is available so it can be used read the ORC file format data, previous example extended below.

Reading and writing ORC file, using format specific method. Exactly the same way you can read ORC data

df.write.mode("overwrite").orc("/tmp/testORC")

#Reading back the stored file using format specific parquet method
orcData= spark.read.orc("/tmp/testORC")
display(orcData)

Reading Data using JDBC sources

Most of you know that in Java or Scala if we need to read the data from the MySQL, Oracle or SQLServer then we use the JDBC and specific driver would be provided and same detail we also need in the Spark to read data from these databases. If during the exam if database connection string is provided then you should know, how we can use it to read the data. Let's see the example for MySQL DB.

About the Database you need to know the three things

-   Hostname: On which database server is hosted
-   Port: to make the connection with the DB
-   Schema/Database name

Once you have these detail you can create JDBC string as below

Example: Making JDBC connection and reading the data using DataFrameReader jdbc method.

```
jdbcDF = spark.read \
  .format("jdbc") \
  .option("url", "jdbc:postgresql:dbserver") \
  .option("dbtable", "schema.tablename") \
  .option("user", "username") \
  .option("password", "password") \
  .load()
```

Another way

```
jdbcDF2 = spark.read \
    .jdbc("jdbc:postgresql:dbserver", "schema.tablename",
        properties={"user": "username", "password":
"password"})
```

Till now, we have not seen any questions being asked for the jdbc method. If you face such question please let us know.

Reading SparkSQL table as DataFrame: Use below method to read Spark SQL table as a DataFrame

SparkSession.table(tableName) :
Returns the specified table as a DataFrame.

Example pseudo code:
```
df.createOrReplaceTempView("table1")
df2 = spark.table("table1")
sorted(df.collect()) == sorted(df2.collect())
```

You can create a table using the DataFrame as well which can be a local or global. This table represent structured data. We can create table from Dataframe using below method, this is a local table.

dataFrame.createOrReplaceTempView("Name_Of_t he_Table")

Example-15: Using table method to read local table

```python
%python

#define a Row object for the Data
HadoopExam = Row("CourseName" , "Location" ,
"CourseFee", "NumberOfStundents" , "Experience" )

#parallelize the collection of Rows and create a DataFrame
using toDF function
heDataFrame = sc.parallelize([
HadoopExam("Hadoop", "Mumbai", 7000, [30, 40, 29],
{"Java" : 7})
,HadoopExam("Spark", "Newyork", 8000, [32, 41, 37],
{"Hadoop" : 4})
,HadoopExam("Machine Learning", "Dubai", 9000, [52, 22,
33], {"Matlab" : 6})
,HadoopExam("Data Science", "Chennai", 11000, [44, 45, 32],
{"SAS" : 12})
,HadoopExam("Cloud Computing", "Hydrabad", 15000, [43,
23, 44], {"Networking" : 8})
]).toDF()

#Show the content of the DataFrame
heDataFrame.show()

#Create the local table using DataFrame
heDataFrame.createOrReplaceTempView("heTable")

heTableDF = spark.sql("select * from heTable")

#Display all the data from DataFrame
```

```
display(heTableDF.select("*"))
```

```
#Using the table method of the SparkSession
heTableDF1 = spark.table("heTable")
display(heTableDF1.select("*"))
```

How to configure options for specific formats

While reading the file using DataframeReader you have to provide some options. For example, in case if you are reading a csv file first thing you need to provide is the path where is the file located it can be on HDFS, S3 or local file system. And your cluster should have permission to access this file from that location. As some method of the DataFrame directly takes the path as an argument and you don't have to separately provide the path to the file.

```
csvDataFrame = dataFrameReader.csv("hedata.csv");
```

There are various other parameters we need to provide like what is the separator in the file. It cannot always be a comma; file can be a pipe separate or tilde separated. Whether file is having first record as header or not. Below is an example of reading a csv file with some of the options.

heDF1 =
spark.read.format("csv").option("header",True).option(
"Inferschema", true).load("HadooExam_Training.csv")

Similarly, there are various options for reading csv file. You should have some practice using them (go to practice exam material on hadoopexam.com) . Some of the other examples are below

- **sep (default ,)**: *sets a single character as a separator for each field and value.*
- **quote (default ")**: *sets a single character used for escaping quoted values where the separator can be part of the value. If you would like to turn off quotations, you need to set not null but an empty string. This behaviour is different from com.databricks.spark.csv.*
- **escape (default \)**: *sets a single character used for escaping quotes inside an already quoted value.*
- **header (default false)**: *uses the first line as names of columns.*
- **inferSchema (default false)**: *infers the input schema automatically from data. It requires one extra pass over the data.*
- **nullValue (default empty string)**: *sets the string representation of a null value. Since 2.0.1, this*

applies to all supported types including the string type.

- **nanValue (default NaN):** sets the string representation of a non-number" value.
- **dateFormat (default yyyy-MM-dd):** sets the string that indicates a date format. Custom date formats follow the formats at java.text.SimpleDateFormat. This applies to date type.
- **timestampFormat (default yyyy-MM-dd'T'HH:mm:ss.SSSXXX):** sets the string that indicates a timestamp format. Custom date formats follow the formats at java.text.SimpleDateFormat. This applies to timestamp type.
- **maxColumns (default 20480):** defines a hard limit of how many columns a record can have.
- **maxCharsPerColumn (default -1):** defines the maximum number of characters allowed for any given value being read. By default, it is -1 meaning unlimited length
- **multiLine (default false):** parse one record, which may span multiple lines.

For exam perspective most of the time you should practice these three formats JSON, CSV and Parquet (Don't miss these three formats).

Reading or loading parquet format: Below is the example, how you read the parquet file.

data = spark.read.parquet("/tmp/testParquet")

Parquet is one of the best file formats for the structured data which has in-built schema. So that you don't have to provide too many options. Below is one of the option which you can use

mergeSchema (default is the value specified in spark.sql.parquet.mergeSchema): *sets whether we should merge schemas collected from all Parquet part-files. This will override spark.sql.parquet.mergeSchema.*

Parquet is the file format which can support Schema Evolution, which is also possible in other file format like Avro, Protocol Buffer and Thrift. It means you start with the simple schema and then later on add more columns to the schema as on when needed. As a side effect in each of your parquet file you would have different number of columns. Let's say as below

- File1.parquet (CourseName, CourseFee)
- File2.parquet (CourseName, CourseFee, Location)
- File3.parquet (CourseName, CourseFee, Location, Trainer)
- File4.parquet (CourseName, CourseFee, Trainer)

So, all above 4 different parquet file has different columns and all files are compatible with each other. Hence, using the parquet method of DataFrameReader for reading all 4 files require schema to be merged and that can be easily enabled as below.

Example-16: Parquet file with *mergeSchema* option (must know for your real exam)

%python

```
#create first partitions
heDF1 = spark.createDataFrame([("Hadoop", 6000), ("Spakr",
5000)]).toDF("CourseName", "CourseFee")
heDF1.show()
heDF1.write.mode("overwrite").parquet("tmp/parquet2/key=
1")

#create second partitions
heDF2 = spark.createDataFrame([("Java", 6000 , "Mumbai"),
("R", 5000, "Pune")]).toDF("CourseName", "CourseFee" ,
"Location")
heDF2.show()
heDF2.write.mode("overwrite").parquet("tmp/parquet2/key=
2")
#create third partitions
heDF3 = spark.createDataFrame([("Java", 6000 , "Mumbai" ,
"Amit"), ("R", 5000, "Pune" , "John")]).toDF("CourseName",
"CourseFee" , "Location" , "Trainer")
```

```
heDF3.show()
heDF3.write.mode("overwrite").parquet("tmp/parquet2/key=
3")

#create fourth partitions
heDF4 = spark.createDataFrame([("Perl", 6000 , "Imran"),
("Oracle", 5000, "Vinod")]).toDF("CourseName", "CourseFee"
, "Trainer")
heDF4.show()
heDF4.write.mode("overwrite").parquet("tmp/parquet2/key=
4")

# Read the ALL partitioned DATA and using the
#mergeSchema command. You should be able to #read #back
#all the file with the all columns
finaleMergedDF = spark.read.option("mergeSchema",
"true").parquet("tmp/parquet2")
finaleMergedDF.printSchema()

finaleMergedDF.show()
```

You can see output schema as below, which has
merged columns from all the files.

```
root
|-- CourseName: string (nullable = true)
|-- CourseFee: integer (nullable = true)
|-- Location: string (nullable = true)
|-- Trainer: string (nullable = true)
|-- key: integer (nullable = true)
```

Options while reading JSON file. In case of JSON also Spark can infer the schema from the data. In case of default, where we don't have option provided than DataFrameReader JSON method consider each individual line as a single JSON object completely and must not span across the line. If you have JSON file which crosses the more than one line than you have to use multiline option as below.

spark.read.option("multiLine", true).json("multiline_he_data_1.json")

Similarly, there are more option which you can decide based on the requirement given and use them.

How to read data from non-core formats using format () and load ()

Till now the method we have seen from the DataFrameReader are format specific like for reading JSON data we are using json() method and similarly to read csv data we are using csv() method of the DataFrameReader. There is one more method which are not format specific which is a format() method, to explicitly specify the format of the data. Below is the example of using format method to read a csv and json file.

#format agnostic load method #Loading csv file
spark.read.format("csv").option("header",true).option("inferS chema",true).load("HadooExam_Training.csv").show()

#Loading json file
#You can specify like json, csv, parquet, orc, text, jdbc etc.
spark.read.format("json").option("header",true).option("infer Schema",true).load("he_data_1.json").show()

And similarly, you can provide various options as well. When you use the format() method on the DataFrameReader then it again return the DataFrameReader and you have to use the load() method to read the data from sources to read the data. As you can see in the above example how we can specify required option as well.

format() method is available on both DataFrameReader and DataFrameWriter to specify the input or output format respectively.

Example: Reading csv data using format method

%python

heDataFrame = spark.read.format("csv").option("header", "true").option("inferSchema", "true").load("diamonds.csv")

heDataFrame.show()

Data Correctness: Handling corrupted records in csv/json file

While reading csv file using DataFrameReader there are option available to handle the corrupted records and these options are below, which can be defined using "mode"

- **PERMISSIVE**: This is a default mode, it means whenever corrupted record is found in data puts the malformed string into a field configured by columnNameOfCorruptRecord, and sets other fields to null. If you want to hold corrupt records than you have to define option as below

spark.read .option("mode", "PERMISSIVE") .option("columnNameOfCorruptRecord", "he_corrupted_records")

In this case it will read corrupted record and keep as part of DataFrame, you have to define "columnNameOfCorruptRecord "as part of custom schema. If a schema does not have the field, it drops corrupt records during parsing. However, in this mode please note that if number of fields are more or less than defined schema. It will not consider that record as corrupt record. If number if fields are less than remaining column will be set as null and if number of tokens are more than it will drop those extra fields.

As we have provided the option "columnNameOfCorruptRecord" , what it does it will keep the corrupted records with under the new column name "he_corrupted_records".

- **DROPMALFORMED:** In this mode corrupted record will be dropped.
- **FAILFAST:** As soon as corrupted record is found; it will throw an exception and also show the corrupted record as part of exception.

There are various options available for reading files and all the common issues are taken care. You can refer the API DOC for all available options. Go to the practice material provided by HadoopExam.com to practice the same example and multiple-choice questions and answers.

How to specify a DDL formatted schema
If you are from the SQL background then you must know what is the DDL. It represents Data Definition Language, so while creating table you provide schema like type of each column. For example,

employee table can be created as below in the Oracle database.

CREATE TABLE employee
(employee_id number(10),
 employee_name varchar2(50),
 location varchar2(50)
);

Somewhat similar you should be able to provide the schema in Spark as well so that SQL developer become comfortable working with the Spark as well.

spark.read.schema("ID INT, Name STRING, Fee DOUBLE").csv("heData.csv")

How to construct and specify a schema using StructType classes

Schema Inference

You can load data from the raw file or any other data sources. While loading the data you can either infer the schema from the data itself. While loading the JSON or csv file you can mention an option as infer schema with values as True and therefore it can infer the schema based on the data. SparkSQL engine, then sample some data to infer the schema from loaded sample data. Let's see an example below, while reading the data using DataFrameReader (spark.read), we are providing options that data is having header as well as infer a schema. However, sometime this approach may not be useful or results in a way it is expected. Because whatever Schema is inferred by SparkSQL engine, you may not wanted that. Hence, you have to explicitly assign a schema to your data, so that it can be structured accordingly.

%python

#format agnostic load method
#Loading csv file
spark.read.format("csv").option("header",True).option("infer Schema",True).load("/FileStore/tables/HadooExam_Training. csv").show()

#Loading json file
#You can specify like json, csv, parquet, orc, text, jdbc etc.
spark.read.format("json").option("header",True).option("infe rSchema",True).load("/FileStore/tables/he_data_1.json").sho w()

Explicitly assigning schema

Example-17: Fetch the schema detail

```
%python

from pyspark.sql import Row

#define a Row object for the Data
HECourse = Row("id" , "name" , "fee", "venue" , "duration" )

#Create an RDD with 5 HECourses
courseRDD = sc.parallelize(
[HECourse(1, "Hadoop", 6000, "Mumbai", 5)
,HECourse(2, "Spark", 5000, "Pune", 4)
,HECourse(3, "Python", 4000, "Hyderabad", 3)
,HECourse(4, "Scala", 4000, "Kolkata", 3)
,HECourse(5, "HBase", 7000, "Banglore", 7)])

#Check the types of RDD
print(courseRDD)

#Convert RDD into DataFrame, as RDD has schema
information, so DataFrame will automatically infer that
schema.
heCourseDF = courseRDD.toDF()

heCourseDF.show()

#Print the schema
heCourseDF.schema

#Print each individual datatype
print(heCourseDF.schema.fields)
```

`heCourseDF.schema.simpleString`

`heCourseDF.schema.fieldNames()`

`heCourseDF.schema.json()`

`heCourseDF.printSchema`

In the above example HECourse is a Row object having five fields. And data also has five fields. We are creating an RDD using these Row objects and then finally converting into DataFrame, so the schema would be preserved which was created using Row objects.

Explicitly creating schema using StructType and StructFields

In this case you will be using StructType and StructField classes to create the schema. StructType will have sequence of StructFields. StructType can be nested as well. For example we can create schema for HECourse as below

Example-18: Creating schema for JSON data

%python

from pyspark.sql.types import ArrayType, StructField, StructType, StringType, IntegerType, LongType, DoubleType

#Create Schema for the JSON data
heschema = StructType([
  StructField("id", LongType(),False),
  StructField("name",StringType(),False),
  StructField("fee", DoubleType(),False),
  StructField("venue", StringType(),False),
  StructField("Duration", LongType(),False)])

#Use defined schema while loading the data
jsonDataDF=spark.read.format("json").schema(heschema).lo ad("/FileStore/tables/he_data_1.json")

jsonData=jsonDataDF.select("name", "fee" , "venue").where(jsonDataDF.fee > 5000)

#Check the output
jsonData.show()

There are many ways by which you can create schema explicitly, see the example below. Once schema is created you can print it in various format like simple String, Tree or JSON format

Example-19: Working with Schema

```python
%python
#Import StructType class and other types
from pyspark.sql.types import ArrayType, StructField,
StructType, StringType, IntegerType, LongType, DoubleType
from pyspark.sql.functions import col
from pyspark.sql import Row
#However, python does not need explicit type information.
#But while defining schema we need to do that. So Catalyst
#Optimizer can use this
#Type information for optimizing the Row
#If values and types does not matched during schema
assignment it will throw error
#Adding the fields to StructTypes one by one
sampleSchema1 = StructType().add("course_id",
IntegerType()).add("course_name",
StringType()).add("course_fee", IntegerType()).add("venue",
StringType())
#Define a course_detail type which can hold upto four
#venues
course_detail = StructType( [StructField("name", StringType(),
True)
                    , StructField("Fee", IntegerType(), False)
                    , StructField("City", StringType(), False)
                    , StructField("Zip", IntegerType(), False)
                    ])
```

```
#Check the structure of the defined schema
print(course_detail.json)
print(course_detail.simpleString)

# Create  Rows instances
row = Row("Hadoop" ,5000,"Mumbai" ,400001 )
row1 = Row("Spark" ,5000,"Pune" ,111045 )
row2 = Row("Cassandra" ,5000,"Banglore" ,530068 )

#Accessing values from Row using ordinal position
print(row(0))
print(row(2))
print(row(3))

#Now create the DataFrame using the schema we have
created above
HEDF=
spark.createDataFrame(spark.sparkContext.parallelize([row,
row1, row2]),course_detail)

#Check whether valid schema is assigned or not
HEDF.printSchema()

#Check the data
HEDF.show()
HEDF.schema
```

When you create or assign schema, it will give structure to your data with the following three things.

- Name of the columns
- Types of the columns
- Nullability (Whether the value of the column can be null or not)

DataFrame will always have schema, where

- At compile time you can assign schema explicitly.

Schema is a StructField, which has collections of StructFields and each StructField represent a column name in a DataFrame.

StructType --> [Collection of StructFields]

You will be using below package

pyspark.sql.types

In SparkSQL, Catalyst SQL parser is responsible for deriving actual datatypes. All the Datatypes information is stored in String format in external catalog. And can be represented as

- Catalog string (the way it is stored in catalog)

- JSON: Compact JSON format of datatype information
- Simple String: Readable string representation for the type.
- Sql string: SQL representation of Datatypes

Values in StructType: Values in StructType

- Represented using Row object.
- A StructType will hold a StructFiled, however StructField can have another StructType in it, which can represent nested or complex Row object.

Download Source code

Write Data to the "core" data formats (csv, json,
jdbc, orc, parquet, text and tables)

DataFrameWriter

To read the data from external data sources we
have used DataFrameReader, similar to this writing
data to external data sources we can use
DataFrameWriter. However, remember that
DataFrameReader was created using SparkSession
object, but DataFrameWriter will be created using
DataFrame.write() method. It's a member of
DataFrame and not SparkSession object.

We have already done various example for writing
the data to external source in previous example,
let's see few more example for the same.

Example-20: Writing data to external source in csv format

%python

#Import StructType class and other types
from pyspark.sql.functions import col
from pyspark.sql import Row

#Loading json file
#You can specify like json, csv, parquet, orc, text, jdbc etc.
heJSONDF =
spark.read.format("json").option("header",True).option("infe
rSchema",True).load("/FileStore/tables/he_data_1.json")

 # DataFrames can be saved as csv files
heJSONDF.write.mode("overwrite").csv("/FileStore/tables/he.
csv")

 # Read in the csv file created above
csvHEDF = spark.read.csv("/FileStore/tables/he.csv")
csvHEDF.show()

csvHEDF.createOrReplaceTempView("csvFile")
*heDF = spark.sql("SELECT * FROM csvFile")*
heDF.select("_c3").show()

Example-21: Writing data to external source in JSON format

%python

```python
#Import StructType class and other types
from pyspark.sql.functions import col
from pyspark.sql import Row

#Loading json file
#You can specify like json, csv, parquet, orc, text, jdbc etc.
heJSONDF =
spark.read.format("json").option("header",True).option("infe
rSchema",True).load("/FileStore/tables/he_data_1.json")

# DataFrames can be saved as JSON files, maintaining the
schema information
heJSONDF.write.mode("overwrite").json("/FileStore/tables/h
e.json")


# Read in the JSON file created above
jsonHEDF = spark.read.json("/FileStore/tables/he.json")
jsonHEDF.show()

jsonHEDF.createOrReplaceTempView("jsonFile")
heDF = spark.sql("SELECT * FROM jsonFile")
heDF.select("name").show()
```

Example-22: Writing data to external source in ORC format

```python
%python

#Import StructType class and other types
```

```python
from pyspark.sql.functions import col
from pyspark.sql import Row

#Loading json file
#You can specify like json, csv, parquet, orc, text, jdbc etc.
heJSONDF =
spark.read.format("json").option("header",True).option("infe
rSchema",True).load("/FileStore/tables/he_data_1.json")

# DataFrames can be saved as ORC files, maintaining the
schema information
heJSONDF.write.mode("overwrite").orc("/FileStore/tables/he.
orc")

# Read in the orc file created above
orcHEDF = spark.read.orc("/FileStore/tables/he.orc")
orcHEDF.show()

orcHEDF.createOrReplaceTempView("orcFile")
heDF = spark.sql("SELECT * FROM orcFile")
heDF.select("name").show()
```

**Example-23: Writing data to external source in Parquet
format**

%python

```python
#Loading json file
#You can specify like json, csv, parquet, orc, text, jdbc etc.
```

```
heJSONDF =
spark.read.format("json").option("header",True).option("infe
rSchema",True).load("/FileStore/tables/he_data_1.json")

# DataFrames can be saved as Parquet files, maintaining the
schema information
heJSONDF.write.mode("overwrite").parquet("/FileStore/table
s/he.parquet")


# Read in the parquet file created above
# Parquet files are self-describing so the schema is preserved
# The result of loading a Parquet file is also a DataFrame
parquetHEDF =
spark.read.parquet("/FileStore/tables/he.parquet")
parquetHEDF.show()

parquetHEDF.createOrReplaceTempView("parquetFile")
spark.sql("SELECT name FROM parquetFile").show()
```

API Methods (API Doc): Currently following API
methods available for DataFrameWriter

- **pyspark.sql.DataFrameWriter(df)** : Interface
  used to write a DataFrame to external storage
  systems (e.g. file systems, key-value stores, etc).
  Use DataFrame.write() to access this.

- **bucketBy**(numBuckets, col, *cols) : Buckets the output by the given columns.If specified, the output is laid out on the file system similar to Hive's bucketing scheme.
numBuckets – the number of buckets to save
col – a name of a column, or a list of names.
cols – additional names (optional). If col is a list it should be empty.

- **csv(String path)** : Saves the content of the DataFrame in CSV format at the specified path.
- **format(source)**: Specifies the underlying output data source.
- **insertInto(tableName, overwrite=False)** : Inserts the content of the DataFrame to the specified table. It requires that the schema of the class:DataFrame is the same as the schema of the table.
- jdbc(url, table, mode=None, properties=None) : Saves the content of the DataFrame to an external database table via JDBC.
- mode(saveMode): Specifies the behavior when data or table already exists.
  - append: Append contents of this DataFrame to existing data.
  - overwrite: Overwrite existing data.

- error or errorifexists: Throw an exception if data already exists.
- ignore: Silently ignore this operation if data already exists.
- json,orc,parquet,text : These all are format specific methods. You can check API doc here.

Other important points for DataFrameReader and DataFrameWriter:
- By default DataFrameReader assumes that input files are parquet files, if it has different format than you have to specify the format explicitly while reading data.
- If you want to change default read format than you have to change the property called "spark.sql.sources.default"

Data Compressions
Spark can read write compressed format, and default compression formats are
1. Lzo
2. Snappy
3. Gzip
4. None
You can specify the compressions as below

dataFrame.write.option("compression" *,*
"None").save("HE_DATA_FILE")

Overwriting existing files

While reading the data we have different modes like pemissive, failFast and dropMalFormed. Similarly, duing the writing the data using DataFrameWrite there is also modes are provided which we can use to decide whether to overwrite an existing file or not.

Using the option method of DataFrameWrite we can provide how to overwrite the existing data. There are following save modes.

- **Append**: We want to keep the existing data and any new data should be appended in the same directory.
- **Overwrite**: If data already existing the directory then using this option you can delete the same. **Remember**: This is explicitly mentioned in the CRT020 certification syllabus. Hence, have a practice for that.
- **error or errorifexists**: This is a good option than mistakenly you would not overwrite existing data. Hence, using this option if file already exists then it can throw an error.

- **Ignore**: If data or directory already exists and you don't want to overwrite as well don't want to through exception/error. Then use this save mode.

By default, errorifexists mode is enabled. Sample syntax is below to use save mode.

heDF.write.format("csv").mode("overwrite").option("sep", "~").save("/heData.csv")

How to configure options for specific formats

Similar to data read using DataFrameReader, we have DataFrameWrite to write data which are specific to native file format like csv, json, parquet, ORC, JDBC, text and tables. All these methods also have option method through which we can specify the options which are specific to a particular format. Like in case of csv, we can provide the separator. Many options we have used while reading the csv data can be used while writing as well. But all may not be possible.

heDF.write.format("csv").mode("overwrite").option("sep", "~").save("/heData.csv")

In above example we have used separator option. Same way we can write the JSON file as well.

heDF.write.format("json").mode("overwrite").save("heData.js on")

Writing parquet file

heDF.write.format("parquet").mode("overwrite").save("/heD ata.parquet")

Similarly, ORC file can have option as below

heDF.write.format("orc").mode("overwrite").save("/heData.o rc")

Writing to RDBMS table

heDF.write.mode("overwrite").jdbc(jdbcConnectionString, "HE_TABLE", props)

How to write a data sources to 1 single or N separate files.

As we have seen till now that Spark provides lot of options to customize while reading or writing data in various format. Whether you use format specific method or general format and load method. Similarly, while working on the DataFrame which you want to save in destination directory. And currently the DataFrame is holding let say 500 partitions and each partition is holding around 100 records. So in total we have 50,000 records. While saving this data we don't want to create 500 small files but rather it should be saved in 50 files.

To accomplish this first we need to merge these 500 partitions into 50 partitions, so while saving DataFrameWriter it would save them in 50 different files. Because for each partition one file would be created. Hence, we can use repartition method to reduce the number of partitions on DataFrame as below

heDF.repartition(50).write.format("csv").save("/tmp/heData.csv")

As we already know that Spark is a Distributed computation engine, where on different data same computation happens on each node in parallel. Part of entire collection of data reside over each node is known as a partition.

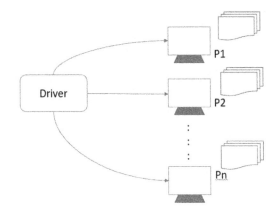

Spark Cluster with DataFrame Partitioning

Data would be partitioned based on the following, to decide what partition strategy to be used:

1. Number of cores in executors
2. Size of the data

Based on above two values, Spark optimizes the parallelism while processing the data. Also, there is a one parameter which decides number of partitions for a DataFrame, which is below.

spark.sql.shuffle.partitions

This parameter is having default value as 200. If you want to change the value in your SparkSession, you can use **spark.conf.set** operator to update this value, similarly other configuration parameters you can change. Here spark is an instance of SparkSession.

If you want to check what all are the partitions are currently available than you have to use below function of the DataFrame.

heDF.rdd.partitions.size()

heDF : It is a DataFrame.

As you can see partitioning is done on the RDD and not directly on the DataFrame object. Hence, we are first retrieving underline RDD of the DataFrame and checking what is the total number of partitions exists for this RDD.

Repartitioning: If you want to re-partition the data than you have to use below operator.

heDF.repartition(x) #Here x, is a number value for partitions to be created

About coalesce operator of DataFrame

This operation results in a narrow dependency, e.g. if you go from 1000 partitions to 100 partitions, there will not be a shuffle, instead each of the 100 new partitions will claim 10 of the current partitions. If a larger number of partitions is requested, it will stay at the current number of partitions.

However, if you're doing a drastic coalesce, e.g. to numPartitions = 1, this may result in your computation taking place on fewer nodes than you like (e.g. one node in the case of numPartitions = 1). To avoid this, you can call repartition(). This will add a shuffle step, but means the current upstream partitions will be executed in parallel (per whatever the current partitioning is).

- This also helps you to re-partition the DataFrame in the given number of partitions.
- Let's see the scenario, what happens If current partitions are more than requested partitions

Current → 5 and Requested → 3 # It will generate new DataFrame with 3 partitions

Current → 5 and Requested → 6# It will remain as 5 partitions only

Example-24: Exercise for Partitions and coalesce functions

%python

```
heDF1 = sc.parallelize([Row(1, "Hadoop", 6000, "Mumbai",
5),Row(2, "Spark", 5000, "Pune", 4),Row(3, "Python", 4000,
"Hyderabad", 3)] , 3).toDF()
```

```
#Check number of partitions

print(heDF1.rdd.getNumPartitions())

#Repartition the DataFrame in 1

heDFNew=heDF1.repartition(1)

#Check number of partitions

#Current number of partitions

print(heDFNew.rdd.getNumPartitions())

#Create a DataFrame with 3 partitions

heDF2 = sc.parallelize([Row(1, "Hadoop", 6000, "Mumbai",
5),Row(2, "Spark", 5000, "Pune", 4),Row(3, "Python", 4000,
"Hyderabad", 3)] , 3).toDF()

#Check number of partitions. Current number of partitions

print(heDF2.rdd.getNumPartitions())

#Repartition the DataFrame in 1

heDFNew2=heDF2.coalesce(1)

#Check number of partitions. Reduces the number of
partitions

print(heDFNew2.rdd.getNumPartitions())

#Repartition the DataFrame in 5

heDFNew3=heDF2.coalesce (5)

#Check number of partitions. It would not increase
```

```
print(heDFNew3.rdd.getNumPartitions())
```

Partitioning and bucketing

While writing data to disk you can decide how to organize the storage so that querying that data would be optimized. Suppose you are getting data on daily basis with high volume, and you query data based on each day to avoid un-necessary disk access you will be creating (Directory structure) partitions for each day as below.

-year=2018/month=01/day=01 -- *This partition for 1st Jan 2018 data*

-year=2018/month=01/day=02 -- *This partition for 2nd Jan 2018 data*

This is same as you do in Hive, hence partitioned written using Spark can be read by Hive as well with the same partition info. So, whenever you query this data back you must use partitioned column as part of predicates in your query, so that you will get the best performance. However, if you have distinct values in tens of thousands then avoid using that column as a partitioned column, because it will create tens of thousands of small files which is not good. So, to choose the partition column very carefully, in above scenario we can see that it will be creating 365 partitions for a year, which is ok if you are storing good amount of data for each day. If data stored on HDFS and you will create huge number of partitions than that would be load for NameNode, because for each file NameNode have an entry and will take more memory to store all the partitions.

If data volume is not high on daily basis than you can partition data based on month rather than day basis. You can use this partitioning scheme for any data JSON, Parquet.

Example-25: Writing Parquet file partitioned

```
%python
heData = [("Hadoop ","Mumbai","Lokesh","M",9000),
    ("Spark ","Banglore","Rahul","M",7000),
    ("Scala ","Newyork","Venkat","M",6000),
    ("Python ","Hydrabad","Jasmin","F",7000),
    ("Java","Dubai","Pooja","F",12000)
    ]
columns = ["coursename","location","name","gender","coursefee"]
#Create DataFrame
heDF = spark.createDataFrame(heData,columns)
heDF.show()
heDF.printSchema()
```

```
#Write DataFrame as parquet file
heDF.write.mode("overwrite").parquet("/FileStore/tables/learner.parquet"
)
#Create DataFrame by reading that Parquet file again
parquetDF = spark.read.parquet("/FileStore/tables/learner.parquet")
#Create a Temporary view or table using Parquet DataFrame
parquetDF.createOrReplaceTempView("ParquetTable")
#Select all the records where coursefee is more than 7000
parquetSQLDF = spark.sql("select * from ParquetTable where coursefee >=
7000 ")
parquetSQLDF.show()
parquetSQLDF.printSchema()
#save data back, wich is partitioned by gender and coursefee
heDF.write.mode("overwrite").partitionBy("gender","coursefee").parquet("
/FileStore/tables/learner2.parquet")
#Read back the partitioned data
parquetDF2 = spark.read.parquet("/FileStore/tables/learner2.parquet")
#Create another temporary table from partitioned data
parquetDF2.createOrReplaceTempView("ParquetTable2")
#Create DataFrame which contains only data where gender is Male and
#Course Fee is more than 7000
heDF2 = spark.sql("select * from ParquetTable2  where gender='M' and
coursefee >= 7000")
#Check the explain plan
heDF2.explain()
#Print the DataFrame Schema
heDF2.printSchema()
#Display DataFrame Contents
display(heDF2)
#Read data from specific partitions
```

```
parqDF3 =
spark.read.parquet("/FileStore/tables/learner2.parquet/gender=M")
parqDF3.show()
```

Example-26: Writing csv file partitioned

```
%python
#Default storage is parquet format
spark.read.text("/FileStore/tables/HadooExam_Training.csv").write.mode("
overwrite").save("/FileStore/tables/HadooExam_Training_1")
#Write as Json format
spark.read.text("/FileStore/tables/HadooExam_Training.csv").write.mode("
overwrite").format("json").save("/FileStore/tables/HadooExam_Training_2
")

#Another way to save as json (format specific method)
spark.read.text("/FileStore/tables/HadooExam_Training.csv").write.mode("
overwrite").json("/FileStore/tables/HadooExam_Training_3")

#Save as table
spark.read.text("/FileStore/tables/HadooExam_Training.csv").write.mode("
overwrite").saveAsTable("T_COURSE")
sql("select * from T_COURSE").show()

#All currently available tables in the catalog
spark.catalog.listTables()

#Saving data using partition by
```

```
spark.read.format("csv").option("header",True).load("/FileStore/tables/Ha
dooExam_Training.csv").write.mode("overwrite").partitionBy("fee").save("/
FileStore/tables/HadooExam_Training_4")

#Inserting data into existing table in catalog
#take count before inserting the data
sql("select * from T_COURSE").count()
spark.read.text("/FileStore/tables/HadooExam_Training.csv").write.insertIn
to("T_COURSE")

sql("select * from T_COURSE").show()
sql("select * from T_COURSE").count()
```

How to bucket data by a given set of columns

Bucketing: As we have seen above partition will
create folder for each partition and store the data
in that folder. If you define bucketing as well than
the based on bucketed column it will create a file.
Let's assume we are storing
courses/books/trainings from HadoopExam.com
watched/visited by each user of daily basis. We will
be defining subscriber_id as a bucketing column.
Bucketing will create equal number of files in a
partition. Suppose we have 100000 subscribers
than inside the folder it may create 4 buckets/files
and each file will be storing 25000 subscriber detail
as below

```
-year=2018/month=01/day=01/bucket_1
-year=2018/month=01/day=01/bucket_2
-year=2018/month=01/day=01/bucket_3
-year=2018/month=01/day=01/bucket_4

-year=2018/month=01/day=02/bucket_1
-year=2018/month=01/day=02/bucket_2
-year=2018/month=01/day=02/bucket_3
-year=2018/month=01/day=02/bucket_4
```

There are lot of advantages when you do the bucketing while sorting on bucketed column, it will be performant. Suppose you are joining two tables with having bucket on the same columns than also it would be performant, because they are joined bucket by bucket. Number of buckets are defined by user and always remain constant.

So, remember for partitioning you should choose the column which does not have very high distinct values e.g. in 10's of thousands and more. But in case of bucketing you should choose a column which has very high cardinality and data can be evenly distributed among the buckets. Again, important point is you need to choose the columns for partitioning and bucketing based on the query you will using on this data.

Writing Parquet file partitioned & Bucketed

```
df.write.format("parquet")
.sortBy("courseName")
.partitionBy("gender")
.bucketBy(4,"fee")
.option("path", "filePath")
.saveAsTable("data.parquet")
```

Chapter-12: DataFrame

Download Source code

http://hadoopexam.com/books/code/4DatabricksSparkPytho
nCRT020/SourceCode.zip

Have a working understanding of every action such
as take(), collect() and foreach()

Transformations & Actions

If you are working on the RDD or DataFrame, you
must know the difference between Transformation
and actions.

Transformation create another DataFrame from the existing DataFrame. As you know DataFrame's are immutable. Hence, you have to apply transformation and that would return a new DataFrame. Some of the common functions you need to know which are transformation and would be used in your data pipeline

- map()
- filter()
- filterMap()
- union()
- intersection()
- distinct()
- groupByKey()
- reduceByKey()
- aggregateByKey()
- sortByKey()
- join()
- cogroup()
- pipe()
- coalesce()

However, this may not be limited in the exam and you may have to use above listed transformations as well. So better go and practice all the questions on the HadoopExam.com . Below is pseudo code for the transformations

heDF.filter(heDF.key >100)

```
heDF.filter(contains("HadoopExam"))
```

However, by this time we have done lot of exercises as well. And you have used these transformations and actions. We have already discussed about the narrow and wide transformations as well.

To initiate the actual transformation which you have already written in a program require an action that is the reason transformation is called lazy. Example of the actions are below

- heDF.count()
- heDF.collect()

Until Spark find the action command in the code, it would be creating a better plan and finally DAG to be executed.

In the certification exam, it is specifically talking about three actions which you know are below

- foreach()
- take()
- collect()

Let's understand them one by one

Foreach: using foreach () action you can iterate over each line of the DataFrame. See example below to print each record from the DataFrame we can use foreach () action.

```
#Print each individual datatype
heCourseDF.foreach(print)
```

Similarly, if you want to print each element from the Row/record, you can use the foreach method as well.

Foreach would be done on all the nodes on the cluster, because your DataFrame is partitioned and available across all the nodes in the cluster. You can use foreach when you want to do some transformation on each individual record in the DataFrame. API definition of foreach method is below

foreach(func): Applies the f function to all Row of this DataFrame. This is a shorthand for df.rdd.foreach(). Runs func on each element of this DataFrame.

map vs foreach function:

Most of the beginner learners are sometime get confused between map and foreach function. Hence, you should know the difference between these two.

map function:
1. map function is a transformation because it returns an RDD by applying function on each element of the RDD. Map function is not directly available on the DataFrame in case

of Python. You have to fetch the RDD and then you can apply map function on RDD.

2. map function iterates over each element or record in the RDD and apply required transformation on each element like converting each record in RDD to uppercase.

3. map is lazy as other transformation; it would not be executed immediately

foreach function:

1. foreach also iterates over each element in the DataFrame.

2. It would be applied immediately

3. Foreach does not return any value.

4. However, on each element of the DataFrame you can apply the function.

5. Foreach is an action.

Collect Action: This is the first or second action you would use when you start programming in Spark. Whenever, you call collect method on the DataFrame, it would return entire records from the DataFrame as an array to the Driver. Assume, if you have a DataFrame which has 50 partitions and each partition has 1000 records in it. Hence, if you call collect method on the DataFrame as below

heDF.collect()

Then it would return 50,000 records to the Driver. So, your driver process should have enough memory to hold so many data else it would through out of memory. Below is another example of iterating all the records in a DataFrame on the driver.

heDF.collect().foreach(println)

Do you think above foreach method is a transformation, no. Because we are iterating over the array and not on the DataFrame. If you are directly calling foreach method on DataFrame then only it is considered as an action.

take () action:

take is also an action and before showing the data it would collect the data to the driver and then result would be presented. However, there is a difference between collect and take. In case of take () method you have to provide how many records you want to fetch. And you should avoid fetching larger number of records, because it can cause OutOfMemory issue. As you can see from below API doc, it returns the Array of Row[] element.

Example-27: Create an example using foreach, collect and take action

%python

```
heList = [1,2,3,4,5]
from pyspark.sql import SparkSession
from pyspark.sql.types import IntegerType

#Create Object of SparkSession
spark = SparkSession.builder.master("local").getOrCreate()
#Remember how you can provide type of the Data
df = spark.createDataFrame(heList, IntegerType())
#df.show()
#Take first 2 record and display it
display(df.take(2))
```

Have a working understanding of the various transformations and how they work such as producing a distinct set, filtering data, repartitioning and coalescing, performing joins and unions as well as producing aggregates.

Producing Distinct Data

Generating distinct values from a DataFrame also known as De-duplicating the data, means remove all the duplicates from the data and get all the distinct records. In this case it can be applicable that you have to get the distinct values across all the columns in a DatFrame or for a few columns in the DataFrame.

To do that DataFrame itself has a one transformation method called distinct() which can be applied to get all the distinct records from the DataFrame. Very simple example as below

heDF.distinct().select(*)

Above command would give you another DataFrame with the same columns but new DataFrame would have only distinct records or rows.

Deduplication is actually removing all the duplicate records from the DataFrame which could be based on all columns or based on few columns. Let's see below hands on example for the same

Example-28: Getting distinct values from the DataFrame

%python

from pyspark.sql import Row

#Define a Row for HadoopExam course detail
HECourse = Row("id", "name", "fee", "venue", "duration")

#Getting distinct rows from DataFrame
heDF = sc.parallelize([
  HECourse(1, "Hadoop", 6000, "Mumbai", 5)
  ,HECourse(2, "Spark", 5000, "Pune", 4)
  ,HECourse(3, "Python", 4000, "Hyderabad", 3)
  ,HECourse(4, "Scala", 4000, "Kolkata", 3)
  ,HECourse(5, "HBase", 7000, "Banglore", 7)
  ,HECourse(4, "Scala", 4000, "Kolkata", 3)
  ,HECourse(5, "HBase", 7000, "Banglore", 7)

```
  ,HECourse(11, "Scala", 4000, "Kolkata", 3)
  ,HECourse(12, "HBase", 7000, "Banglore", 7)]).toDF()
```

#Getting distinct values from DataFrame
```
heDF.distinct().show()
```

#Remove duplicates using selected columns
```
heDF.dropDuplicates(["name","fee","venue","duration"]).show()
```

#Removing all the common rows from a DataFrame
```
heDF2= sc.parallelize([HECourse(1, "Hadoop", 6000, "Mumbai", 5)
                ,HECourse(2, "Spark", 5000, "Pune", 4)
                ,HECourse(3, "Python", 4000, "Hyderabad", 3)]).toDF()
```

#except will remove all the rows from heDF which are present in heDF2
#and also gives unique rows #from heDF
```
heDF.exceptAll(heDF2).show()
```

Filtering Data:

When you need to filter the data, you have to use
Booleans or function which returns either true and
false. There are mainly two ways you apply the
filter on the DataFrame either using the filter
function or where function.

Example-29: In continuation with the previous example, lets apply the filter function

#Using filter function
```
heDF.filter(heDF.fee>6000).show()
```

#Define a Row for HadoopExam course detail

```
HECourse = Row("id", "name", "fee", "venue", "duration")

#Create an RDD with 5 HECourses records.
courseRDD = sc.parallelize([
  HECourse(1, "Hadoop", 6000, "Mumbai", 5)
  ,HECourse(2, "Spark", 5000, "Pune", 4)
  ,HECourse(3, "Python", 4000, "Hyderabad", 3)
  ,HECourse(4, "Scala", 4000, "Kolkata", 3)
  ,HECourse(5, "HBase", 7000, "Banglore", 7)])

#Check the types of RDD
print(courseRDD)

#Convert RDD into DataFrame, as RDD has schema information, #so
DataFrame will automatically
#infer that schema. As HECourse Row is used to create DataFrame,
#it will be using this Row to infer the schema.
heCourseDF = courseRDD.toDF()

#Select the courses conducted in Mumbai, having price more than 5000
#Also, you can select the columns, you need (It is DSL or programming
interface)
filteredDF = heCourseDF.where("fee
>5000").where("venue=='Mumbai'").select("name","fee", "duration")
filteredDF.show()
```

Example-30: Using expressions

%python

from pyspark.sql import Row
from pyspark.sql.functions import expr

#expr function, you will be passing any expression
#in String to this function and based on this data can be filtered.
#You can even use Row to create DataFrame
#Define a Row for HadoopExam course detail
HEEmployee= Row("ID", "Name", "gender", "Salary", "Department")

```
HEEmployeeDF = sc.parallelize([
  HEEmployee(1, "Deva", "Male", 5000, "Sales"),
  HEEmployee(2, "Jugnu", "Female", 6000, "HR"),
  HEEmployee(3, "Kavita", "Female", 7500, "IT"),
  HEEmployee(4, "Vikram", "Male", 6500, "Marketing"),
  HEEmployee(5, "Shabana", "Female", 5500, "Finance"),
  HEEmployee(6, "Shantilal", "Male", 8000, "Sales"),
  HEEmployee(7, "Vinod", "Male", 7200, "HR"),
  HEEmployee(8, "Vimla", "Female", 6600, "IT"),
  HEEmployee(9, "Jasmin", "Female", 5400, "Marketing"),
  HEEmployee(10, "Lovely", "Female", 6300, "Finance"),
  HEEmployee(11, "Mohan", "Male", 5700, "Sales"),
  HEEmployee(12, "Purvish", "Male", 7000, "HR"),
  HEEmployee(13, "Jinat", "Female", 7100, "IT"),
  HEEmployee(14, "Eva", "Female", 6800,"Marketing"),
  HEEmployee(15, "Jitendra", "Male", 5000, "Finance"),
  HEEmployee(15, "Rajkumar", "Male", 4500, "Finance"),
  HEEmployee(15, "Satish", "Male", 4500, "Finance"),
  HEEmployee(15, "Himmat", "Male", 3500, "Finance")], 2).toDF()

#Check the data in DataFrame
HEEmployeeDF.show()

#Now create an expression. These expressions are Column types.
#Since you use interactive session all objects are defined in the same scope
#and become a part of the closure.

maleExpr = expr("gender='Male'")
emaleExpr= expr("gender='Female'")
salExpr= expr("Salary >=6600")

#Now apply these filters to the data
HEEmployeeDF.filter(maleExpr).show()
HEEmployeeDF.filter(femaleExpr).show()
HEEmployeeDF.filter(salExpr).show()
```

Repartitioning DataFrame: If you want to re-partition the data than you have to use below operator.

heDF.repartition(x) #Here x, is a number value for partitions to be created

Partitioning of the Data actually affects the physical layout of the across the cluster. You know this is very important for the optimization of your program that you should do the DataFrame partitioning based on the frequently filtered columns. When we apply the re-partitioning on the DataFrame it applies full data shuffling the cluster based on the partition key columns.

As suggested, we should re-partition the DataFrame only when after re-partitioning we are expecting a greater number of partitions or we have specific requirement where we need to partition the data based on the specific columns.

To get to know what are the current number of partitions then use the following commands on the DataFrame

heDF.rdd.getNumPartitions()
To change the number of partitions, use the below command

heDF.repartitions(20)

If we know that you would be having most of the queries based on specific columns then partition it based on the columns as below

heDF.repartition(10, col("course_name"))

Coalescing the DataFrame: It is considered as a typed transformation of a DataFrame.

- This also helps you to re-partition the DataFrame in the given number of partitions.
- Let's see the scenario, what happens If current partitions are more than requested partitions

  Current → 5 and Requested → 3 *# It will generate new DataFrame with 3 partitions*

  Current → 5 and Requested → 6 *# It will remain as 5 partitions only*

As a general rule you should use the coalesce() function to reduce the number of partitions. Coalesce does not perform the shuffle as it is being done in repartition. And when you save your DataFrame in a file, it may create as many numbers of files as number of partitions. But each partition may not have equal amount of data.

Repartition:

1. When you want all the future partitions to have equally distributed chunks.
2. If you want a greater number of partitions
3. It would have data shuffling to create the required number of partitions.

Coalesce:

1. When you want to reduce the number of partitions.
2. Avoid shuffling

Less number of partitions also affects the parallelism; hence you should have well balanced number of partitions based on the cluster capacity.

Exercise for Partitions and coalesce functions

Example-31: Partitions and coalesce functions

%python

```
#Create a DataFrame with 3 partitions
HECourse = Row("id", "name", "fee", "venue", "duration")

heDF1 = sc.parallelize([HECourse(1, "Hadoop", 6000, "Mumbai",
5),HECourse(2, "Spark", 5000, "Pune", 4),HECourse(3, "Python", 4000,
"Hyderabad", 3)] , 3).toDF()

#Check number of partitions
print(heDF1.rdd.getNumPartitions())

#Repartition the DataFrame in 1
heDFNew1=heDF1.repartition(1)
```

```
#Check number of partitions
print(heDFNew1.rdd.getNumPartitions())

#Create a DataFrame with 3 partitions
heDF2 = sc.parallelize([HECourse(1, "Hadoop", 6000, "Mumbai",
5),HECourse(2, "Spark", 5000, "Pune", 4),HECourse(3, "Python", 4000,
"Hyderabad", 3)] , 3).toDF()

#Check number of partitions
heDF2.rdd.getNumPartitions()

#Repartition the DataFrame in 1
heDFNew2=heDF2.coalesce (1)

#Check number of partitions
print(heDFNew2.rdd.getNumPartitions())

#Repartition the DataFrame in 5
heDFNew3=heDF2.coalesce (5)

#Check number of partitions
print(heDFNew3.rdd.getNumPartitions())
```

Joins in the DataFrame:

A Join is a way to retrieve information from two or
more DataFrames. There are various types of joins.
A normal JOIN, which is also called an INNER JOIN, a
LEFT OUTER JOIN, a RIGHT OUTER JOIN, a FULL
OUTER JOIN and CROSS JOIN.

SQL Example of inner join

Suppose a you wanted to know what employee
worked in what department. While someone could

just compare the ID numbers between the two tables, a way to have the information in one place is by doing a JOIN, also known as an INNER JOIN. Because they have one type of data in common, the department ID, the tables can be joined together.

SELECT LastName, DepartmentName FROM employee join department on department.DepartmentID = employee.DepartmentID;

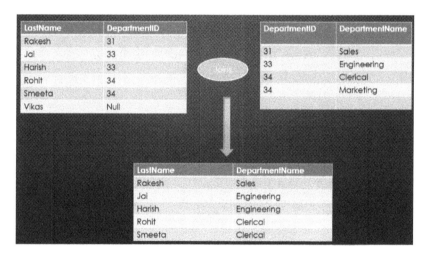

SQL Inner Join example

Outer Joins: Inner joins are fine if both tables have a matching record. However, if one table does not have a record for what the join is being built on, the query will fail. But if a database programmer needs to grab information in an event that there is not a matching record for a row on one of the tables, they need to use an outer join. Types of outer joins are

- Left
- Right
- Full outer join
- Cross Joins

We will be doing joins example using SparkSQL. However, concept for joining DataFrame in SparkSQL and tables in SQL Databases are same. So if you have ever done this things in RDBMS then it would be quite easy for you.

Explanation for

- *Left Join*: A left outer join (also known as a left join) will contain all records from the left DataFrame, even if the right DataFrame does not have a matching record for each row.
- *Right Join*: A right outer join works almost like a left outer join, except with how the DataFrames are handled reversed. This time, all of the relevant information will be returned from the right DataFrame, even if the left table does not have a matching result. If the left DataFrame does not have a matching result, null will be in the place of the missing data.

- *Full outer join*: The FULL OUTER JOIN return all records when there is a match in either left DataFrame or right DataFrame records.
- *Cross Join*: The CROSS JOIN produces a result set which is the number of rows in the first DataFrame multiplied by the number of rows in the second DataFrame if no WHERE clause is used along with CROSS JOIN. This kind of result is called as Cartesian Product.

Spark Joins Hands on Exercises:

Example-32: Spark SQL DataFrame Joins

%python

```
#Let's create two DataFrames
heDF1 = spark.read.format("csv").option("header",True).option(
"Inferschema", True).load("/FileStore/tables/HadooExam_Training.csv")
heDF1.show()

#Create another DataFrame
heDF2= sc.parallelize([ Row(1, "Hadoop", 6000, "Mumbai", 5), Row(2,
"Spark", 5000, "Pune", 4), Row(3, "Python", 4000, "Hyderabad",
3)]).toDF(["ID","Name","Fee","City","Days"])
heDF2.show()

#Inner Join
heDF1.join(heDF2, "ID").show()

#Left Join
heDF1.join(heDF2, "ID" , "left_outer").show()
```

```
#Right Join
heDF1.join(heDF2, "ID" , "right").show()

#Full outer Join
heDF1.join(heDF2, "ID" , "fullouter").show()

from pyspark.sql.functions import broadcast
#Broadcast Join using function
print("Show broadcast join")
heDF1.join(broadcast(heDF2), "ID").show()

#Define a Row for HadoopExam course detail
#Using Join operator
HECourse = Row("id", "name", "fee", "venue", "duration")

heDF3 = sc.parallelize([
  HECourse(1, "Hadoop", 6000, "Mumbai", 5),
  HECourse(2, "Spark", 5000, "Pune", 4),
  HECourse(3, "Python", 4000, "Hyderabad", 3) ,
  HECourse(4, "Scala", 4000, "Kolkata", 3),
  HECourse(5, "HBase", 7000, "Banglore", 7) ,
  HECourse(4, "Scala", 4000, "Kolkata", 3),
  HECourse(5, "HBase", 7000, "Banglore", 7) ,
  HECourse(11, "Scala", 4000, "Kolkata", 3),
  HECourse(12, "HBase", 7000, "Banglore", 7)]).toDF()

heDF4 = sc.parallelize([
HECourse(1, "Hadoop", 6000, "Mumbai", 5),
HECourse(2, "Spark", 5000, "Pune", 4),
HECourse(3, "Python", 4000, "Hyderabad", 3)]).toDF()


#Now apply the join operation, it will help you to provide the required
conditions
#apply inner join
resultDF1 = heDF3.join(heDF4 , heDF3.id == heDF4.id)
resultDF1.show()
resultDF1.printSchema()
```

```
#apply Left join with the conditions
resultDF2 = heDF3.join(heDF4 , heDF3.id == heDF4.id , "left")
resultDF2.show()
resultDF2.printSchema()

#apply right join with the conditions
resultDF2 = heDF3.join(heDF4 , heDF3.id == heDF4.id , "right")
resultDF2.show()
resultDF2.printSchema()
```

Unions among DataFrame:

UNION function is used to combine the two or more DataFrames. To do the union

- Each DataFrame must have same number of columns
- Order of the columns should be same in all the DataFrame
- This is for appending the DataFrames.
- In case of Spark (not same as RDBMS), union does not remove the duplicate records from the DataFrame

In case of Spark union and unionall (deprecated) functions are same. If you want to remove all the duplicate records after the union transformation then apply the distinct function on the resultant DataFrame

Example-33: Find the price based on City as well and more on GroupBy operations

%python

#Load the data
heDF1 = spark.read.format("csv").option("header",True).option(
"Inferschema",
True).load("/FileStore/tables/HadooExam_Training_double.csv")

#Select the total price for each Course and Venue
#It is important you import sum function, you remove import statement
and you would see
#It uses in-built sum function and keep giving error.
from pyspark.sql.functions import sum
feeForVenueAndCourse=heDF1.groupBy("Name","Venue").agg(sum('Fee').
alias('TotalFee')).select("Name" , "TotalFee")

#Select the total price for each Venue
feeForVenue=heDF1.groupBy("Venue").agg(sum("Fee").alias("TotalFee"))

#Select the total price for each Course
feeForCourse=heDF1.groupBy("Name").agg(sum("Fee").alias("TotalFee"))

#Now show all the prices together using Union
#Here, you see union needs same number of columns.
#It does not matter whether column names are same or not
#DataFrame "feeForVenue" has different column name as "venue"
from pyspark.sql.functions import desc_nulls_first
feeForVenueAndCourse.union(feeForVenue).union(feeForCourse).sort(desc
_nulls_first("TotalFee")).show()

Aggregation functionality in DataFrame:

GroupedData: Whenever you apply group by function on DataFrame it will return GroupedData, it is little different and you cannot directly apply action API on it. You have to apply some aggregate function on this GroupedData to get the results, you cannot directly print the contents of GroupedData for example

feeForCourse=heDF1.groupBy("Name").agg(sum("Fee").alias("TotalFee"))

These are the below operators of the DataFrame which return GroupedDat. We will discuss all these operators in detail in next section.

- Group By
- Rollup
- Cube
- Pivot

Multi Dimension aggregations

There are two operators which can help you get the total, sub-total and grand total and they are known as multi-dimension operators, which are below

- Rollup
- Cube

Remember:

- You cannot print or collect GroupedData.
- Calling count() on grouped DataFrame is a transformation and not considered as an

action. Hence, you have to call the collect method on the result.

DataFrame Aggregation API

Aggregation API will help in working with the group of data and applying aggregations on it. In database management an aggregate function is a function where the values of multiple rows are grouped together to form a single value of more significant meaning or measurement such as a set, a bag or a list.

Group by clause is used to group the results of a SELECT query or Select API call on DataFrame based on one or more columns. It is also used with SQL functions to group the result from one or more tables.

Let's check various aggregate functions, aggregate functions require the group by clause, if you want to apply aggregations on subset of rows else aggregations will be done on entire DataFrame.

Example-34: Various aggregations and caching example

%python

#Lets create a DataFrame
heDF = spark.read.format("csv").option("header",True).option(
"Inferschema", True).load("/FileStore/tables/HadooExam_Training.csv")

```python
#Register as a temp table
heDF.createOrReplaceTempView("T_HECOURSE")

#Cache the table
sql("CACHE TABLE T_HECOURSE")

#Check the storage page UI and must be there as an In Memory table
#https:#community.cloud.databricks.com/?o=8715781396654982#/setting
/clusters/1117-052927-tube192/sparkUi

#You can also check whether table is cached or not
spark.catalog.isCached("T_HECOURSE")

sql("CACHE TABLE T_HECOURSE")

#Clear the cache
sql("CLEAR CACHE")

#Import Required Storage level
from pyspark import StorageLevel

#Defining storage level, by default it is MEMORY_ONLY
spark.catalog.cacheTable("T_HECOURSE")

#It is required, you call this to cache the table
sql("SELECT * FROM T_HECOURSE").show()

sql("CLEAR CACHE")

#Applying aggregate using SQL query, quite easy, we should #be able to do
this using DataFrame API
spark.sql("SELECT SUM(FEE), Venue FROM T_HECOURSE GROUP BY
venue").show()

#Lets calculate entire fee collected
from pyspark.sql.functions import sum
heDF.agg(sum("fee").alias("TotalFee")).show()
```

```
#Now calculate the fee for each venue
heDF.groupBy("venue").agg(sum("fee").alias("TotalFee")).show()

#Calculate average fee
from pyspark.sql.functions import avg
heDF.groupBy("venue").agg(avg("fee").alias("TotalFee")).show()

#Calculate max fee
from pyspark.sql.functions import max,min,avg,count
heDF.groupBy("venue").agg(max("fee").alias("TotalFee")).show()

#Course count for each city using groupByKey
print("Counting records based on venue")
heDF.groupBy("venue").count().show()

#Now calculate more than one aggregation altogether
heDF.groupBy("venue").agg(sum("fee").alias("TotalFee") , max("fee") ,
min("fee") , count("fee"), avg("fee") ).show()
```

Another example of group by operations

Example-35: Find the price based on City as well and more on GroupBy operations

```
%python
```

```
#Load the data
heDF1 = spark.read.format("csv").option("header",True).option(
"Inferschema",
True).load("/FileStore/tables/HadooExam_Training_double.csv")
```

```
#Select the total price for each Course and Venue
feeForVenueAndCourse=heDF1.groupBy("Name","Venue").agg(sum("Fee").
alias("TotalFee")).select("Venue" , "Name" , "TotalFee")
```

```
#Select the total price for each Venue
from pyspark.sql.functions import lit
feeForVenue=heDF1.groupBy("Venue").agg(sum("Fee").alias("TotalFee"
)).select("Venue" , lit("Total Price from this Venue").alias("Name") ,
"TotalFee")
feeForVenue.show()

#Select the total price for each Course
feeForCourse=heDF1.groupBy("Name").agg(sum("Fee").alias("TotalFee")
).select(lit("Total Price from this Course").alias("Venue") , "Name" ,
"TotalFee")

#Now show all the prices together using Union
feeForVenueAndCourse1=heDF1.groupBy("Name","Venue").agg(sum("Fee"
).alias("TotalFee")).select("Venue" ,"Name" , "TotalFee")

feeForVenue1=heDF1.groupBy("Venue").agg(sum("Fee").alias("TotalFee")).
select("Venue" , lit("Total Price from this Venue").alias("Name") ,
"TotalFee")

feeForCourse1=heDF1.groupBy("Name").agg(sum("Fee").alias("TotalFee")
).select(lit("Total Price from this Course").alias("Venue") , "Name" ,
"TotalFee")

from pyspark.sql.functions import asc_nulls_last,asc_nulls_first
feeForVenueAndCourse1.union(feeForVenue1).union(feeForCourse1).sort(a
sc_nulls_last("Venue")).show()
feeForVenueAndCourse1.union(feeForVenue1).union(feeForCourse1).sort(a
sc_nulls_first("Venue")).show()

#Save the result and you can check
feeForVenueAndCourse1.union(feeForVenue1).union(feeForCourse1).sort(a
sc_nulls_last("Venue")).write.mode("overwrite").format("csv").save("/FileS
tore/tables/HadooExam_Training_GroupBy_csv")

#Let's try to do the same operation using SQL query
```

```python
heDF2 = spark.read.format("csv").option("header",True).option(
"Inferschema",
True).load("/FileStore/tables/HadooExam_Training_double.csv")

#Register temp view
heDF2.createOrReplaceTempView("T_HEDATA")

#Desired SQL Query
#Grouping Set is equivalent of Union of each Group by operations
#Which will provide total as well as grand total
heGroupByDataFrame = sql("""
  SELECT Venue, COALESCE(Name, "Total price per venue") as Name,
SUM(Fee) as TotalFee
  FROM T_HEDATA
  GROUP BY Venue, Name
  GROUPING SETS ((Venue, Name), (Venue))
  ORDER BY Venue ASC NULLS LAST, Name ASC NULLS LAST
  """)

print("Grouped Data Output")
heGroupByDataFrame.show()

#Grouping Set is equivalent of Union of each Group by operations
#Which will provide total as well as grand total
heGroupByDataFrame1 = sql("""
  SELECT Venue, COALESCE(Name, "Total price per venue") as Name,
SUM(Fee) as TotalFee
  FROM T_HEDATA
  GROUP BY Venue, Name
  GROUPING SETS ((Venue, Name), (Venue),())
  ORDER BY Venue ASC NULLS LAST, Name ASC NULLS LAST
  """)

#Check the data values
heGroupByDataFrame1.show()

#Save the datavalues
```

```
heGroupByDataFrame1.repartition(1).write.mode("overwrite").format("csv
").save("/FileStore/tables/HadooExam_Training_groupingset")

#Grouping Set is equivalent of Union of each Group by operations
#Which will provide total as well as grand total
#Result similar to cube
#We created separate DataFrame for this (Check for HE Spark and total
and subtotal)
heDF3 = spark.read.format("csv").option("header",True).option(
"Inferschema",
True).load("/FileStore/tables/HadooExam_Training_double_1.csv")

#Register temp view
heDF3.createOrReplaceTempView("T_HEDATA")

heGroupByDataFrame2 = sql("""
  SELECT Venue, COALESCE(Name, "Total price per venue") as Name,
SUM(Fee) as TotalFee
  FROM T_HEDATA
  GROUP BY Venue, Name
  GROUPING SETS ((Venue, Name), (Venue),(Name) , () )
  ORDER BY Venue ASC NULLS LAST, Name ASC NULLS LAST
  """)

#Check the data values
heGroupByDataFrame2.show()

#Save the datavalues
#You should get total price of all the courses
#Total price for each individual course
#Total Price for combination of Venue and Course
heGroupByDataFrame2.repartition(1).write.mode("overwrite").format("csv
").save("/FileStore/tables/HadooExam_Training_groupingset_3")
```

Know how to cache the data, specifically to disk, memory or both.

DataFrame operations which does not fall in either Transformations or actions: SparkSQL DataFrame has some operations which does not fall in either transformations or actions like Cache, persist etc. Let's see the example below for such methods.

Exercise-36: Various DataFrame operators or functions example, which are not transformations or actions

%python

```
#Load the data
heDF1 = spark.read.format("csv").option("header",True).option(
"Inferschema",
True).load("/FileStore/tables/HadooExam_Training_double.csv")

#Lets create a DataFrame
heDF = spark.read.format("csv").option("header",True).option(
"Inferschema", True).load("/FileStore/tables/HadooExam_Training.csv")

#Cache the DataFrme( MEMORY_AND_DISK)
heDF1.cache()

#You can check, about this cached data (Ip of your Spark host)
#https:#community.cloud.databricks.com/?o=8715781396654982#/setting
/clusters/1117-052927-tube192/sparkUi

#It should not, yet cached
#Now call action, so calculation will happen and all the transformations will
be called
```

#Which can result in caching the DataFrame
#After that check the above web page by refreshing it
heDF1.count()

#check whether DataFrame is cached or not in Spark-shell itself
print(heDF1.is_cached)

#Un-persist the data
heDF1.unpersist()

#Now check the storage page
#https:#community.cloud.databricks.com/?o=8715781396654982#/setting
/clusters/1117-052927-tube192/sparkUi

#check whether DataFrame is cached or not in Spark-shell itself
print(heDF1.is_cached)

#Check the execution plan of next select statement so that, you will get to
know about InMemory DataFrame
heDF.select("ID", "Name").explain(True)

#Checkpoint DataFrame, it should throw exception, as you have not set the
checkpoint dir
#heDF.checkpoint()

#Lets set the checkpoint dir (Directory will be created)
spark.sparkContext.setCheckpointDir("/FileStore/tables/checkpoint")

#Converting DataFrame to DataFrame
heDF1.show()

#Rename the columns
heDF1.toDF("CourseId","CourseName","CourseFee","CourseVenue","Course
Date","CourseDuration").show()

#Un-persisting the RDD
heDF1.unpersist()

Cached Data in Spark Storage UI

Caching the DataFrame will help future operations to complete much faster, because it does not have to calculate the DataFrame again, and for any future calculation it will use the cached DataFrame. (For caching and checkpointing, we will have separate dedicated chapter). Caching operation itself is not a transformation or action but DataFrame will be cached only after you call action on DataFrame. Once DataFrame is cached, you can open Spark UI and can check under the storage tab whether DataFrame was persisted or not. There is an API option also available to check whether DataFrame is persisted or not as below.

heDF1.is_cached

If you don't need DataFrame further, you can drop the cached DataFrame using unpersist method on the DataFrame.

Know how to uncache previously cached data

DataFrame and Caching

As you know, if we want to use the transformation output in later step of calculations, then you cache an RDD, which saves time in future steps. Similarly, DataFrame can be cached. But again, DataFrames are more efficient than RDD, DataFrame will take lesser space compare to RDD to store the same amount of data why? Because DataFrame already know the types of each elements/attributes and take advantage of this. So that while caching them optimally layout the DataFrame and save the memory space. Even, DataFrame has Encoders which helps in further reducing the space consumed by DataFrame by providing detailed information of the JVM objects.

SparkSQL and Caching: We can cache the RDD in Core Spark, similarly in SparkSQL DataFrame can be cached. Caching will give advantages only when DataFrame are used more than once in an application. If there is no re-use of DataFrame and DataFrame then it is wastage of memory. So, it is always better to un-persist the DataFrame, if it is not used further (Timely un-persisting is an optimization technique in SparkSQL).

DataFrame.unpersist() #un-persisting a DataFrame

Sometime you see when you try to cache a DataFrame, your application may crash. Reason, what type of caching you have configured and size of DataFrame. Suppose size of the DataFrame is quite bigger and not enough memory is available than application will crash. And also caching parameters configured one is "MEMORY_ONLY". Change this configuration to "MEMORY_AND_DISK". By doing this you are able to persist bigger DataFrame as well, even memory space is limited. Because with this configuration, whatever data which does not fit in memory will be saved.

Converting a DataFrame to a global or temp view

You can create table or views from the DataFrame and the advantages of doing that is you can run the SQL query on this tables and if you are comfortable with that then this is one of the best things to do.

When you create the temporary views then these are session specific and once your session is killed then this temp views are also deleted. If there is a requirement that views should be shared across the sessions then you should create global temporary views and you have to keep your application in which these are created. One another important thing is that this global temporary views are tied to a specific database schema which is controlled by Spark system known as global_temp. Hence, while selecting data from global temp view, you need to use

SELECT * FROM global_temp.heView

There are multiple ways by which you can create global temporary views as below.

heDF.createOrReplaceTempView("heTempView")
heDF.createGlobalTempView("heGlobalTempView")

In the first command you are creating or replacing existing temp view which is local to the session. As soon as your SparkSession is terminated, this view is also dropped. If you want to explicitly drop that view then use the below command

spark.catalog.dropTempView("heTempView")

And if you want to drop the Global Temporary view then use the below command

```
spark.catalog.dropGlobalTempView("heGlobalTempView")
```

Example-37: Create local and global temporary view

%python

#Loading data from multiple files into DataFrame
jsonDataTwoFiles=
spark.read.format("json").load(["/FileStore/tables/he_data_1.json","/FileSt ore/tables/he_data_2.json"])

#Check the types of data
jsonDataTwoFiles.show()

#To check whether DataFrame is local or not, it means when you run the collect and take methods,
#it check this DataFrame is available locally. Hence, no need to run the executor on worker node if return true.
jsonDataTwoFiles.isLocal()

#Returns all the columns of DataFrames
jsonDataTwoFiles.columns

#Columns with their datatypes
jsonDataTwoFiles.dtypes

#Schema for the DataFrame
jsonDataTwoFiles.schema

#Global view v/s local view
jsonDataTwoFiles.createOrReplaceTempView("V_HELOCAL1")
jsonDataTwoFiles.createOrReplaceGlobalTempView ("V_HEGLOBAL1")

#Select data from both the views
*sql("select * from V_HELOCAL1").show()*

```
sql("select * from global_temp.V_HEGLOBAL1").show()
```

Applying hints: SparkSQL and Hint

While running the SQL query using Spark SQL you can provide the hint and hint will help the optimizer correct plan to execute your query. Hint are used while optimizing the logical plan. You can apply hint to query as well as DataFrame API

Hints are currently available only for the join operation.

Example-38: Joins with the hints

```
%python
```

```
#Lets create a DataFrame
heDF1 = spark.read.format("csv").option("header",True).option(
"Inferschema", True).load("/FileStore/tables/HadooExam_Training.csv")
```

```
#Lets create a DataFrame
heDF2 = spark.read.format("csv").option("header",True).option(
"Inferschema",
True).load("/FileStore/tables/HadooExam_Learners_stats.csv")
```

```
#Do the joins and apply hint as broadcast
heDF1.join(heDF2.hint("broadcast"), "ID")
```

```
#Check whether hint is resolved or not
heDF1.join(heDF2.hint("broadcast"), "ID").explain()
```

```
#Parameter to check current smaller file size threshold
print(spark.conf.get("spark.sql.autoBroadcastJoinThreshold"))
```

However, as part of Spark 2.4 release they have increased support for the hints as well and you can provide the hints the query as well. And the hints you provide in the query can help Spark System to optimize the logical query plan and optimizer can use hint to optimize the query. Now there is more support introduced for hint as below, we have already seen the BROADCAST hint, similarly for COALESCE and REPARTITIONS hints are added. If your hints are not resolved then they would be removed.

It depends that you are using DataFrame or Spark SQL query and you can provide hint accordingly as below

Example : Using hint with the DataFrame

```
heDF= createDataFrame()
hintedDF = heDF.hint(name = "heHint", 100, true)
hintedDF.queryExecution.logical

Example-33: Hint in the SQL query
#Reduce the number of partitions hint
SELECT /*+ COALESCE(10) */ course_name , course_fee from
heDFTable
```

```
#Increase the number of partitions hint
SELECT /*+ REPARTITION(100) */ course_name , course_fee
from heDFTable

#Similarly below you can apply
SELECT /*+ MAPJOIN(b) */

SELECT /*+ BROADCASTJOIN(b) */

SELECT /*+ BROADCAST(b) */
```

Chpater-13 Section-10: Spark SQL Functions

Download Source code

http://hadoopexam.com/books/code/4DatabricksSparkPytho
nCRT020/SourceCode.zip

Access to Certification Preparation Material
I have already purchased this book printed version from
open market, I still wanted to get access for the
certification preparation material offered by
HadoopExam.com, do you provide any discount for the
same.
Answer: First of all, thanks for considering the learning
material from HadoopExam.com. Yes, we certainly

Aggregate functions: getting the first or last item from an array or computing the min and max values of a columns.

DataFrame Aggregation API

Aggregation API will help in working with the group of data and applying aggregations on it. In database management an aggregate function is a function where the values of multiple rows are grouped together to form a single value of more significant meaning or measurement such as a set, a bag or a list.

Group by clause is used to group the results of a SELECT query or Select API call on DataFrame based on one or more columns. It is also used with SQL functions to group the result from one or more tables.

Let's check various aggregate functions, aggregate functions require the group by clause, if you want to apply aggregations on subset of rows else aggregations will be done on entire DataFrame.

Example-39: Using explode function

%python

#Sample data in a file "HE_TRAINING.json"
#{"Hadoop":6000,"City":["Mumbai","Hyderabad"]}

#We wanted to convert this data in file as below.
#Hadoop,City
#6000,Mumbai
#6000,Hyderabad

#We can do it using below Collection function of DataFrame

from pyspark.sql.functions import explode

#Load JSON data as a DataFrame
heTraining= spark.read.json("/FileStore/tables/HE_TRAINING.json")

heTraining.show()

#We need to flatten the data in a City for each Training course
heTrainingCityFee= heTraining.withColumn("City", explode("City"))
heTrainingCityFee.show()

About explode function

It is very similar, as we have used with the RDD. It will create a new Row for each value or element in a given array or Map. In above DataFrame City is an array with the two values in it. [Mumbai. Hyderabad]. Which will be generating new row for each city.

```
SELECT explode(array("Spark", "Hadoop" , "Scala"));
```

It would generate a new DataFrame with 3 new rows in it as below

> Spark
> Hadoop
> Scala

Data time functions: parsing strings into timestamps or formatting timestamps into strings

As name suggests these are the functions for working on the time and dates manipulation. Please see the below example for Date and Time function.

Example-40: Various Date Time and window Functions

%python

#This all functions are part of package
from pyspark.sql.functions import explode

#Lets do some arithmatic function on date and timestamp using sql
#Substract date by 1 day
spark.sql("select date_sub(current_timestamp(), 1)").show()

```
#Get current date
spark.sql("select current_date() ").show()

#add days
spark.sql("select date_add(current_date() , 2)").show()
#substract days
spark.sql("select    date_sub(current_date() , 2)").show()

#add months
spark.sql("select add_months(current_date() , 2)").show()
#Difference between two dates (Current date - current date+2 months)
spark.sql("select datediff(current_date() , add_months(current_date() ,
2))").show()

#Getting the last day of the months
spark.sql("select    last_day(current_date()) ").show()
#Getting the hour part
spark.sql("select hour(current_timestamp())").show()
#Extract month part
spark.sql("select month(current_timestamp())").show()
#Getting number of months between two dates
spark.sql("select    months_between(add_months(current_date() , 2),
current_date())").show()
#Get the quarter of the date
spark.sql("select quarter(current_timestamp())").show()
from pyspark.sql.functions import current_timestamp,hour,last_day
#Getting similar output from DataFrames API
spark.range(1).select(current_timestamp()).show()
spark.range(1).select(hour(current_timestamp())).show()
spark.range(1).select(last_day(current_timestamp())).show()

from pyspark.sql.functions import date_format
#Date Formatting
spark.range(1).select(date_format(current_timestamp(), "dd-MMM-
yyyy")).show()
spark.range(1).select(date_format(current_timestamp(), "dd-MMM-yyyy
hh:mm:ss")).show()
```

```
spark.range(1).select(date_format(current_timestamp(), "dd-MMM-yyyy
hh:mm:ss")).show()

#Getting unix timestamp (Also known as unix epoc timestamp)
from pyspark.sql.functions import unix_timestamp
spark.range(1).select(unix_timestamp()).show()

#This way any column of DataFrame you can convert into Date Datatype
from pyspark.sql.functions import to_date,lit
spark.range(1).select(to_date(lit("2018-07-27"))).show()

#Creating window with slide duration.
spark.sql("select window(current_timestamp() ,'5 minutes' , '1
minutes')").take(20)

from pyspark.sql import Row

heCourses = sc.parallelize([
Row(1, "2018-01-01", 20000),
Row(1, "2018-01-02", 23000),
Row(1, "2018-01-03", 90000),
Row(1, "2018-01-04", 55000),
Row(1, "2018-01-05", 20000),
Row(1, "2018-01-06", 23000),
Row(1, "2018-01-07", 90000),
Row(1, "2018-01-08", 55000),
Row(2, "2018-01-01", 80000),
Row(2, "2018-01-02", 90000),
Row(2, "2018-01-03", 100000),
Row(2, "2018-01-04", 80000),
Row(2, "2018-01-05", 90000),
Row(2, "2018-01-06", 100000),
Row(2, "2018-01-07", 80000),
Row(2, "2018-01-08", 90000)
])

from pyspark.sql.functions import col
```

```
heCoursesDF=spark.createDataFrame(heCourses , ["course_id",
"start_date" , "fee"]).withColumn("start_date",
col("start_date").cast("date"))

heCoursesDF.show()
```

```
# calculating the total fee every day across courses
from pyspark.sql.functions import window,sum
totalFeeEveryDay = heCoursesDF.groupBy(window("start_date", "1
days")).agg(sum("fee").alias("total_fee")).select("window.start",
"window.end", "total_fee")
totalFeeEveryDay.orderBy("start").show()
```

```
#Total fee collected in every two day
totalFeeEvery2ndDay = heCoursesDF.groupBy(window("start_date", "2
days")).agg(sum("fee").alias("total_fee")).select("window.start",
"window.end", "total_fee")
totalFeeEvery2ndDay.orderBy("start").show()
```

Math functions: converting a value to crc32, md5, sha1 or sha2

Non-aggregate functions: creating an array, testing if a column in null, not-null, nan etc.

By looking at below exercise you can see few of the selected non-aggregate functions. For example

- **array** --> Creates a new array column. The input columns must all have the same data type.
- **expr** --> Parses the expression string into the column that it represents.

- **struct** --> Creates a new struct column that composes multiple input columns.
- **monotonically_increasing_id** --> A column expression that generates monotonically increasing 64-bit integers. The generated ID is guaranteed to be monotonically increasing and unique, but not consecutive. The current implementation puts the partition ID in the upper 31 bits, and the record number within each partition in the lower 33 bits. The assumption is that the data frame has less than 1 billion partitions, and each partition has less than 8 billion records.

Example-41: Some more utility functions

- **expr**
- **array**
- **struct**
- **monotonically_increasing_id**

```
#expr function, you will be passing any expression in String to this function
and based on this data can be filtered.
#You can even use Row to create DataFrame
#Define a Row for HadoopExam course detail
HEEmployee =Row("ID", "Name", "gender", "Salary", "Department")

HEEmployeeDF = sc.parallelize([HEEmployee(1, "Deva", "Male", 5000,
"Sales"), HEEmployee(2, "Jugnu", "Female", 6000, "HR"), HEEmployee(3,
"Kavita", "Female", 7500, "IT"), HEEmployee(4, "Vikram", "Male", 6500,
"Marketing"), HEEmployee(5, "Shabana", "Female", 5500, "Finance"),
HEEmployee(6, "Shantilal", "Male", 8000, "Sales"), HEEmployee(7, "Vinod",
```

"Male", 7200, "HR"), HEEmployee(8, "Vimla", "Female", 6600, "IT"),
HEEmployee(9, "Jasmin", "Female", 5400, "Marketing"), HEEmployee(10,
"Lovely", "Female", 6300, "Finance"), HEEmployee(11, "Mohan", "Male",
5700, "Sales"), HEEmployee(12, "Purvish", "Male", 7000, "HR"),
HEEmployee(13, "Jinat", "Female", 7100, "IT"), HEEmployee(14, "Eva",
"Female", 6800,"Marketing"), HEEmployee(15, "Jitendra", "Male", 5000,
"Finance")
, HEEmployee(15, "Rajkumar", "Male", 4500, "Finance")
, HEEmployee(15, "Satish", "Male", 4500, "Finance")
, HEEmployee(15, "Himmat", "Male", 3500, "Finance")], 2).toDF()

#Check the data in DataFrame
HEEmployeeDF.show()

from pyspark.sql.functions import expr

#Now create an expression. These expressions are Column types.
maleExpr = expr("gender='Male'")
femaleExpr= expr("gender='Female'")
salExpr= expr("Salary >=6600")

#Now apply these filters to the data
HEEmployeeDF.filter(maleExpr).show()
HEEmployeeDF.filter(femaleExpr).show()
HEEmployeeDF.filter(salExpr).show()

from pyspark.sql.functions import array

#Now lets create array by combining multiple columns in DataFrame and
drop the same column from output
HEEmployeeDF.filter(salExpr).withColumn("Array" ,
array("Name","gender", "Department")).drop("Name","gende",
"Department").show()

from pyspark.sql.functions import struct

#Now lets create array by combining multiple columns in DataFrame and
drop the same column from output

```
HEEmployeeDF.filter(salExpr).withColumn("Struct" ,
struct("Name","gender", "Department")).drop("Name","gende",
"Department").show()

#Even both support mixed datatypes as well
HEEmployeeDF.filter(salExpr).withColumn("Array" ,
array("Name","gender", "Department")).drop("gender", "Department",
"Salary").show()
HEEmployeeDF.filter(salExpr).withColumn("Struct" ,
struct("Name","gender", "Department")).drop("gender", "Department",
"Salary").show()


#monotonically_increasing_id()
#Lets create data with 4 partitions
HEEmployeeDF1 = sc.parallelize([HEEmployee(1, "Deva", "Male", 5000,
"Sales"), HEEmployee(2, "Jugnu", "Female", 6000, "HR"), HEEmployee(3,
"Kavita", "Female", 7500, "IT"), HEEmployee(4, "Vikram", "Male", 6500,
"Marketing"), HEEmployee(5, "Shabana", "Female", 5500, "Finance"),
HEEmployee(6, "Shantilal", "Male", 8000, "Sales"), HEEmployee(7, "Vinod",
"Male", 7200, "HR"), HEEmployee(8, "Vimla", "Female", 6600, "IT"),
HEEmployee(9, "Jasmin", "Female", 5400, "Marketing"), HEEmployee(10,
"Lovely", "Female", 6300, "Finance"), HEEmployee(11, "Mohan", "Male",
5700, "Sales"), HEEmployee(12, "Purvish", "Male", 7000, "HR"),
HEEmployee(13, "Jinat", "Female", 7100, "IT"), HEEmployee(14, "Eva",
"Female", 6800,"Marketing"), HEEmployee(15, "Jitendra", "Male", 5000,
"Finance")
, HEEmployee(15, "Rajkumar", "Male", 4500, "Finance")
, HEEmployee(15, "Satish", "Male", 4500, "Finance")
, HEEmployee(15, "Himmat", "Male", 3500, "Finance")], 4).toDF()

# Now generate monotonically_increasing_id() for each row.
#It is a 64 bit integers
#Generated ID must be unique and increasing only.
#It can not be consecutive
#The current implementation puts the partition ID in the upper 31 bits, and
the record number within each partition in the lower 33 bits.
```

```
#The assumption is that the data frame has less than 1 billion partitions,
and each partition has less than 8 billion records.
from pyspark.sql.functions import monotonically_increasing_id
HEEmployeeDF1.withColumn("unique_id",
monotonically_increasing_id()).show()
```

Sorting functions: sorting data in descending order, ascending order, and sorting with proper null handling.

This function will be used to sort the data. We will be using these functions in some other full-length exercises in other section of the book. Below is the list of functions, which falls under this category are (API Doc)

asc(columnName: String):	Returns a sort expression based on ascending order of the column. **Example**: df.sort(asc("dept"), desc("age"))
asc_nulls_last(columnName: String)	Returns a sort expression based on ascending order of the column, and null values appear after non-null

	values. Example: df.sort(asc_nulls_last(" dept"), desc("age"))
desc(columnName: String)	Returns a sort expression based on the descending order of the column. **Example**: df.sort(asc("dept"), desc("age"))
desc_nulls_first(column Name: String)	Returns a sort expression based on the descending order of the column, and null values appear before non-null values. **Example**: df.sort(asc("dept"), desc_nulls_first("age"))
def desc_nulls_last(column Name: String)	Returns a sort expression based on the descending order of the column, and null values appear after

	non-null values. **Example:** df.sort(asc("dept"), desc_nulls_last("age"))
asc_nulls_first(columnN ame: String)	Returns a sort expression based on ascending order of the column, and null values return before non-null values. **Example:** df.sort(asc_nulls_last(" dept"), desc("age"))

String functions: employing a UDF function

As other programming language these functions are used to manipulate the string. We will not go into detail of this function, please refer the API doc for understanding and each individual function. Example of the few functions under this category are below.

1. **concat** : Concatenates multiple input columns together into a single column. If all inputs are binary, concat returns an output as binary. Otherwise, it returns as string.

2. **initcap**: Returns a new string column by converting the first letter of each word to uppercase.
3. **length**: Computes the character length of a given string or number of bytes of a binary string.

These all are trivial and self-explanatory functions, if you have experience with any other programming language than similar functions you would have found with them.

Window functions: computing the rank or dense rank.

Lead and Lag are part of a class of functions called window functions. When you write a query, as the SparkSQL processes each row, lead will look ahead at the next row in the result set in the context of the current row being processed. Lag will look behind in the result set to the row that was processed. However, it is not necessary that you look only just next (in case of lead) or previous (in case of lag) rows. Rather by defining length you can check values in next n rows (in case of lead) or previous n rows values (in case of lag). Let's see an example for lead and lag function to understand the functionality.

Example-42: Exercise: Lead and Lag Function

```
#To use the various functions, we may have to import sql functions
from pyspark.sql import functions

#You can check the available number of functions
print(len(spark.catalog.listFunctions()))

#Window partition ranked function
HEEmployee = Row("ID", "Name", "gender", "Salary", "Department")

HEEmployeeDF = sc.parallelize([ HEEmployee(1, "Deva", "Male", 5000,
"Sales"), HEEmployee(2, "Jugnu", "Female", 6000, "HR"), HEEmployee(3,
"Kavita", "Female", 7500, "IT"), HEEmployee(4, "Vikram", "Male", 6500,
"Marketing"), HEEmployee(5, "Shabana", "Female", 5500, "Finance"),
HEEmployee(6, "Shantilal", "Male", 8000, "Sales"), HEEmployee(7, "Vinod",
"Male", 7200, "HR"), HEEmployee(8, "Vimla", "Female", 6600, "IT"),
HEEmployee(9, "Jasmin", "Female", 5400, "Marketing"), HEEmployee(10,
"Lovely", "Female", 6300, "Finance"), HEEmployee(11, "Mohan", "Male",
5700, "Sales"), HEEmployee(12, "Purvish", "Male", 7000, "HR"),
HEEmployee(13, "Jinat", "Female", 7100, "IT"), HEEmployee(14, "Eva",
"Female", 6800,"Marketing"), HEEmployee(15, "Jitendra", "Male", 5000,
"Finance")
, HEEmployee(15, "Rajkumar", "Male", 4500, "Finance")
, HEEmployee(15, "Satish", "Male", 4500, "Finance")
, HEEmployee(15, "Himmat", "Male", 3500, "Finance")]).toDF()


#Create a Window based on the Gender to rank their salary
#For the same salary it will assign same rank
from pyspark.sql.window import Window
from pyspark.sql.functions import desc_nulls_last
genderPartitionedSpec =
Window.partitionBy("gender").orderBy(desc_nulls_last("Salary"))
```

```
#Lag function will help you find the previous value in the same column
from pyspark.sql.functions import lag
HEEmployeeDF.withColumn("previousValue", lag("Salary",
1).over(genderPartitionedSpec)).show()

#How to find previous second last value in a column
HEEmployeeDF.withColumn("previousValue", lag("Salary",
2).over(genderPartitionedSpec)).show()


#Similarly, third last and increase the range as per need
HEEmployeeDF.withColumn("previousValue", lag("Salary",
3).over(genderPartitionedSpec)).show()

#Get the difference between previous value and current value
HEEmployeeDF2=HEEmployeeDF.withColumn("previousValue",
lag("Salary", 1).over(genderPartitionedSpec))
HEEmployeeDF2.select("ID", "Name", "gender", "Department",  "Salary",
"previousValue", expr("Salary-previousValue").alias("SalaryDiff")).show()

#Now opposite of that using lead function
from pyspark.sql.functions import lead
HEEmployeeDF.withColumn("lead", lead("Salary",
1).over(genderPartitionedSpec)).show()
HEEmployeeDF.withColumn("leadBy2", lead("Salary",
2).over(genderPartitionedSpec)).show()
```

Examples of rank and dense_rank functions (Window function)

dense_rank() : This function returns the rank of each row within a result set partition, with no gaps in the ranking values. The rank of a specific row is one plus the number of distinct rank values that come before that specific row.

rank(): Returns the rank of each row within the partition of a result set. The rank of a row is one plus the number of ranks that come before the row in question. Please note that there is a little difference between rank and dense_rank function, dense_rank will give continuous ranking values if more than one record has same rank, but in case of rank it will produce a gap. Refer the example below to understand in detail. For in-depth definition of similar function refer this MS doc

Example-43: Apply Various Rank Functions on DataFrame

```
#To use the various functions, we may have to import sql functions
from pyspark.sql import functions

#You can check the available number of functions
print(len(spark.catalog.listFunctions()))

#Window partition ranked function
HEEmployee = Row("ID", "Name", "gender", "Salary", "Department")

HEEmployeeDF = sc.parallelize([ HEEmployee(1, "Deva", "Male", 5000,
"Sales"), HEEmployee(2, "Jugnu", "Female", 6000, "HR"), HEEmployee(3,
"Kavita", "Female", 7500, "IT"), HEEmployee(4, "Vikram", "Male", 6500,
"Marketing"), HEEmployee(5, "Shabana", "Female", 5500, "Finance"),
HEEmployee(6, "Shantilal", "Male", 8000, "Sales"), HEEmployee(7, "Vinod",
"Male", 7200, "HR"), HEEmployee(8, "Vimla", "Female", 6600, "IT"),
HEEmployee(9, "Jasmin", "Female", 5400, "Marketing"), HEEmployee(10,
"Lovely", "Female", 6300, "Finance"), HEEmployee(11, "Mohan", "Male",
```

5700, "Sales"), HEEmployee(12, "Purvish", "Male", 7000, "HR"),
HEEmployee(13, "Jinat", "Female", 7100, "IT"), HEEmployee(14, "Eva",
"Female", 6800,"Marketing"), HEEmployee(15, "Jitendra", "Male", 5000,
"Finance")
, HEEmployee(15, "Rajkumar", "Male", 4500, "Finance")
, HEEmployee(15, "Satish", "Male", 4500, "Finance")
, HEEmployee(15, "Himmat", "Male", 3500, "Finance")]).toDF()


```
#Create a Window based on the Gender to rank their salary
#For the same salary it will assign same rank
from pyspark.sql.window import Window
from pyspark.sql.functions import desc_nulls_last, rank
genderPartitionedSpec =
Window.partitionBy("gender").orderBy(desc_nulls_last("Salary"))
HEEmployeeDF.withColumn("rank",
rank().over(genderPartitionedSpec)).show()
```

```
#Create a Window based on the Department to rank their salary
departmentPartitionedSpec =
Window.partitionBy("Department").orderBy(desc_nulls_last("Salary"))
HEEmployeeDF.withColumn("rank",
rank().over(departmentPartitionedSpec)).show()
```

```
#Create a Window based on the Departrment as well as gender to rank
their salary
departmentGenderPartitionedSpec = Window.partitionBy("Department",
"gender").orderBy(desc_nulls_last("Salary"))
HEEmployeeDF.withColumn("rank",
rank().over(departmentGenderPartitionedSpec)).show()
```

```
#Lets get percent rank
#For the same salary it will assign same rank
genderPartitionedSpec1 =
Window.partitionBy("gender").orderBy(desc_nulls_last("Salary"))
from pyspark.sql.functions import percent_rank
HEEmployeeDF.withColumn("percentRank",
percent_rank().over(genderPartitionedSpec1)).show()
```

NTILE (Window) function: **Distributes the rows in an ordered partition into a specified number of groups. The groups are numbered, starting at one. For each row, NTILE returns the number of the group to which the row belongs.**

row_number() function : Numbers the output of a result set. More specifically, returns the sequential number of a row within a partition of a result set, starting at 1 for the first row in each partition.

Exercise-44: Some other useful window based functions

```
#To use the various functions, we may have to import sql functions
from pyspark.sql import functions
```

```
#You can check the available number of functions
print(len(spark.catalog.listFunctions()))
```

```
#Window partition ranked function
HEEmployee = Row("ID", "Name", "gender", "Salary", "Department")
```

```
HEEmployeeDF = sc.parallelize([ HEEmployee(1, "Deva", "Male", 5000,
"Sales"), HEEmployee(2, "Jugnu", "Female", 6000, "HR"), HEEmployee(3,
"Kavita", "Female", 7500, "IT"), HEEmployee(4, "Vikram", "Male", 6500,
```

"Marketing"), HEEmployee(5, "Shabana", "Female", 5500, "Finance"),
HEEmployee(6, "Shantilal", "Male", 8000, "Sales"), HEEmployee(7, "Vinod",
"Male", 7200, "HR"), HEEmployee(8, "Vimla", "Female", 6600, "IT"),
HEEmployee(9, "Jasmin", "Female", 5400, "Marketing"), HEEmployee(10,
"Lovely", "Female", 6300, "Finance"), HEEmployee(11, "Mohan", "Male",
5700, "Sales"), HEEmployee(12, "Purvish", "Male", 7000, "HR"),
HEEmployee(13, "Jinat", "Female", 7100, "IT"), HEEmployee(14, "Eva",
"Female", 6800,"Marketing"), HEEmployee(15, "Jitendra", "Male", 5000,
"Finance")
, HEEmployee(15, "Rajkumar", "Male", 4500, "Finance")
, HEEmployee(15, "Satish", "Male", 4500, "Finance")
, HEEmployee(15, "Himmat", "Male", 3500, "Finance")]).toDF()

```
from pyspark.sql.functions import desc_nulls_last
genderPartitionedSpec =
Window.partitionBy("gender").orderBy(desc_nulls_last("Salary"))
from pyspark.sql.functions import row_number
HEEmployeeDF.withColumn("rowNumber",
row_number().over(genderPartitionedSpec)).show()
```

```
#Select ntile (Various percentire)
#If we divide salary in 3 quartile than in which quartile it fall
from pyspark.sql.functions import ntile
HEEmployeeDF.select("*",
ntile(3).over(genderPartitionedSpec).alias("ntile")).show()
```

```
#Divide with 25% and see in which 25%, employee salary false
HEEmployeeDF.select("*",
ntile(4).over(genderPartitionedSpec).alias("ntile")).show()
```

You can find various exercises before your real
exam in the HadoopExam Spark CRT020
certification material. As it is not possible to add all
the examples in this book. We highly recommend
that you complete all the multiple-choice questions
and answers as well as hands on exercise before

your real exam. Please visit this page to get more detail about this certification. If you are using Hard Copy of the book then go to HadoopExam.com for more detail.

Note: If you have purchased this book on http://hadoopexam.com then all future edition of the same book would be freely available.

Thank you & All the best for your career.

www.ingramcontent.com/pod-product-compliance
Lightning Source LLC
LaVergne TN
LVHW041209050326
832903LV00021B/538